Grace
Rules

Steve McVey
Author of *Grace Walk*

HARVEST HOUSE PUBLISHERS
Eugene, Oregon 97402

Cover by Terry Dugan Design, Minneapolis, Minnesota

GRACE RULES

Copyright © 1998 by Steve McVey
Published by Harvest House Publishers
Eugene, Oregon 97402

Library of Congress Cataloging-in-Publication Data

McVey, Steve, 1954–
    Grace rules / Steve McVey.
       p.   cm.
    ISBN 1-56507-897-7
    1. Salvation. 2. Grace (Theology) 3. Christian life. I. Title.
  BT751.2.M38   1998
  234—dc21   98-12643
                                               CIP

Printed in the United States of America.

07 08 09 10 11 / BP / 14 13 12 11 10 9

To my parents,
with love and appreciation
for laying a godly foundation
in my life.

ACKNOWLEDGMENTS

Grace Rules couldn't have been written without the encouragement and support of numerous people. Special thanks to Bob Hawkins, Jr. for his passion about God's grace and his belief in this book. He and the wonderful staff at Harvest House are a pleasure to work with because to them, it's not only a business, but a ministry.

Thanks to my dear friend and administrator, Stephen Knoblock, who handled a thousand ministry details so I could be free to write. Though often quietly serving behind the scenes, he has been a strong force in spreading the message of the grace walk.

I also feel deep gratitude to Bud and Colette Stokes, and Dianne Sager and her managers and staff, all of who are key people in our ministry. My faith has grown because of the scope of their faith.

I am grateful to my children for their constant support. How blessed I am to be encouraged by Drew, David, Amber, and Amy and her husband, Cliff. And Hannah, our new grand daughter—just to look at her is a testimony of God's wonderful grace. (If you don't believe it, I have pictures available!)

For 25 years my most precious grace gift has been my wife, Melanie. Always the encourager, she has often clarified my spiritual vision when my focus was distracted or distorted. She has been my spiritual advisor, my best friend, and my soul mate.

Above all I give thanks to Jesus Christ, whose life has transformed me and still teaches me what it means to enjoy a life where grace rules. To Him be all the glory for any good that may result from this book.

CONTENTS

1
Living
for Jesus

OPENING HIS EYES, Jesus could see the early morning light beginning to filter in through the window of the small guest bedroom where He had spent the night. He could hear His friend already in the kitchen preparing breakfast. No doubt about it—the mother of all buffets was being prepared. Martha always put out a great spread of food. He loved being in the home of these two sisters and their brother. For a moment He wished He could take the day off and spend some time with them. *It would be nice,* He thought, *but the devil never takes a day off. And besides, My Father is counting on Me.*

Arising from the comfort of the bed, Jesus began to mentally organize His day. *What shall I do for My Father today?* He pondered. *I know that I'll preach a sermon this afternoon. That's one thing that would cause Father to really be happy with Me.* As He washed His face with a wet cloth, He continued, *There are many sick people in the area. I'll heal some of them. My Father would certainly be pleased with that. Maybe I'll even cast out some demons today.*

That's always a big ministry event. When He finished dressing, He thought, *Maybe if all goes well, I can even find a funeral service and raise somebody from the dead. Yes. That's what I'll do. Father will be thrilled when He sees Me take on that ministry project. Those things should pretty much fill My day.* Slipping on His sandals just before walking out of the bedroom to face the new day, He prayed, "Help Me, Father, as I live for You today. Use what I do for You to bring glory to Yourself."

A Reality Check

What are your thoughts on that scenario describing how Jesus might have begun a new day? If it sounds pretty good to you, I implore you, don't put down this book until you have finished reading it. I assume you know that I have described this imaginary scene with tongue in cheek. Nobody would imagine Jesus living His life in such a way. Jesus trying to score brownie points with His Father? There's no way.

Yet for many years I began my own day in a similar way. I arose each morning focusing on all the things that I planned to do for God during the day. I believed that Christians were saved to serve, and I certainly wanted to fulfill the purpose of my salvation. So I dedicated myself to serving Jesus. I was diligent and sincere and often felt successful at it. With my Bible in one hand and my Day Timer™ in the other, I went forward to make my mark for God in this heathen world.

I was a pastor for over 20 years and I was serious about it. My life was dedicated to serving Jesus. My behavior wasn't always consistent, but my desire was. I wanted to live for Him. Even when I didn't think that I was doing a good job living for Him, I still wanted it. I believed that all Christians should live for Jesus and that, as a pastor, it was my calling to tell them how to do it. However, I did notice that no matter how much I did for Jesus, I felt an internal "To Do List" hanging over my head. Serving Jesus was gratifying, but I wouldn't have called it satisfying because I always felt a need to do more.

After I had been a Christian for 29 years, the Lord showed me something that shocked me. I'll tell you what He showed me, but I must first warn you to brace yourself for this. It may have the same shocking effect on you. In fact, if you didn't have any problems with the first few paragraphs of this chapter, you had better have a tongue depressor ready before you read the next statement because you may need it.

God Doesn't Need Us to Serve Him

God doesn't need us to serve Him. What a blow to human pride! I have heard it said that we are the *only* hands that God has, we are the *only* feet that He has, and we are His *only* eyes, ears, and mouth. That's a scary thought. Jesus said that, if necessary, the rocks could cry out praise to Him. God once used a donkey to deliver a message to a prophet. While it's true that the Bible teaches that Christians are the body of Christ, we find ourselves in a precarious situation if we suggest that God's eternal agenda hinges on the actions of human beings. When looking at the modern church, a person could conclude that God is a quadriplegic if we were to say that the mobility of His agenda depends on us serving Him.

The Bible says in Acts 17:25, "Neither is He served by human hands, as though He needed anything, since He Himself gives to all life and breath and all things." God doesn't need us. If you believe otherwise, I encourage you to take an honest inventory of all your abilities and assets and then compare those to the omnipotence of a God who stood on the vast edge of nothingness and said, "Let there be!" and there was. Stop reading and think about that for a moment. Now, what was it you have that God needs?

If you are troubled by the news that God doesn't need us, let me give you a word you will be glad to hear. The good news is that God *wants* us. He has set His love on us and has a desire to enjoy intimacy with us. While I used to believe that Christians are saved to serve, Jesus gave a different reason for God giving us eternal life. In a prayer to His Father, He said, "This is eternal life, that they may know Thee, the only true God, and Jesus Christ whom Thou has sent" (John 17:3). Jesus said that the reason we have been saved is so that we may *know* Him and His Father intimately.

When we focus on our performance,
Christian service becomes
perfunctory and lifeless.
When we are obsessed with Him,
our service is literally
energized with divine life.

Ron and Mary Beth sat in my office, both totally exasperated. "I don't know what she wants," he said. "I do everything I can to make her happy and nothing satisfies her." "Ron, I've told you the problem," she answered softly. "She says that she doesn't feel that I need and appreciate her," he went on. "She knows I need her. I couldn't run my business without her," Ron answered, looking to me for understanding. "That's just the problem," she answered. Turning to me, she said, "I'm nothing more than an administrative assistant to him. I don't have any doubt that he needs what I do in our family business, but he doesn't act like he needs *me*."

Mary Beth's problem illustrates well the misconception that many Christians have about their relationship with God. They believe that their relationship with the Lord revolves around what they do for Him. They feel no intimacy with God because they think His primary interest is in what they can do for Him. While Mary Beth was partly right in her perception of her husband, any Christian who believes that his service to God is the basis of his relationship to the Lord is totally wrong.

When the concept of our relationship to God is service-oriented, we will relate to Him as a divine Employer who scrutinizes our activity to make sure it is up to standard. Our focus will be on our performance as we attempt to do the things we believe He requires. This mindset reflects a legalistic view of the Christian life, a view that's erroneous. God doesn't want us to focus on our service to Him. When grace rules our lives, we focus on Him. In doing so, we experience intimacy in such a way that service becomes a natural overflow of the love relationship we have with Him. When we focus on our performance, Christian service becomes perfunctory and lifeless. When we are obsessed with Him, our service is literally energized with divine life.

Jesus Never Did One Thing for God

I once read a church sign which stated, "Your life is God's gift to you. What you do with it is your gift to God." Nothing could be further from the teaching of the Bible. If we could make something out of our lives, there would be no need for Christ to give Himself to us and take up residence in us when we are saved. It really strokes our human ego to think that we can do something for God. Yet the truth is that we cannot. Only God can do something for Himself. In His infinite grace, He allows us to participate in what He is doing by placing His life inside us and then expressing that life through us. If we aren't operating in that mode, then all that we do adds up to zero.

How did Jesus live in this world? Didn't He do some great things for God? He did not. Jesus came to reveal His Father to the world, but He didn't accomplish that goal by His own strength and ability. Jesus once had a conversation with Philip which clearly shows how He functioned as a man in this world. John 14:8-10 records:

> Philip said to Him, "Lord show us the Father, and it is enough for us." Jesus said to him, "Have I been so long with you, and yet you have not come to know Me, Philip? He who has seen Me has seen the Father; how do you say, 'Show us the Father'? Do you not believe that I am in the Father, and the Father is in Me? The words that I say to you I do not speak on my own initiative, but the Father abiding in Me does His works."

Allow me to paraphrase and amplify that passage: Philip said to Jesus, "Lord, You sure talk a lot about Your Father. Why don't You just let us see Him and we will be satisfied?" Jesus answered him and said, "Philip, you don't have a clue, do you? Have I been with you this long and you still don't get it? If you have seen Me, you have seen the Father. Why are you asking Me to show you the Father? Don't you know that My Father and I are in total union together? Philip, the words that you hear me speak aren't My words. My Father is speaking those words through Me. As for the things you see Me do, it's not Me doing those things. It is My Father, who is inside Me, who does those works."

Jesus very clearly stated that He was not the source of His own words and works. In John 14:24, He said about His speech that "the word which you hear is not Mine, but the Father's who sent Me." It was the Father—who is one with Jesus—who animated Jesus' life.

For centuries theologians have debated what is called the "kenosis" theory in an attempt to explain the relationship between the humanity and deity of Jesus. The word comes from the Greek verb *kenoo*, which means "to empty or divest." When Jesus came into this world, He willingly emptied Himself of divine prerogatives. While retaining 100 percent of His deity, He chose not to live as God, but as a man who depended completely on God the Father. It is true that He was still God while He was on the earth, but he functioned totally as a man. He wanted to make it perfectly clear that He was a man just like us.

If the earthly life of Jesus can be described in terms of His Godhood, it offers us little encouragement. We could simply look at Jesus' lifestyle and say, "Well, of course He lived like that. After all, He is God!" Again, I emphasize that it is important to understand that the life of Jesus can't be explained only because of His deity. Let me put it another way: Do you know how many miracles Jesus could have done if it hadn't been His Father within Him doing the works? Not one. He couldn't have done a thing. Jesus could only do what God the Father was doing *through* Him. Don't take my word for it; listen to what

Jesus Himself had to say about it: "Truly, truly, I say to you, the Son can do nothing of Himself, unless it is something He sees the Father doing; for whatever the Father does, these things the Son also does in like manner" (John 5:19). Jesus said that He could do nothing. Only as the Father expressed His powerful life through the Son did anything happen. Jesus didn't do one thing for God. Instead, He recognized His union with the Father, and God did everything Himself, through Jesus.

Jesus repeatedly asserted that His behavior didn't flow from Himself. He did nothing independent of His Father—*nothing*. Consider Jesus' words in the following examples taken from the gospel of John:

- "I can do nothing on My own initiative" (John 5:30).

- "My teaching is not Mine, but His who sent Me" (John 7:16).

- "I do nothing on My own initiative, but I speak these things as the Father taught Me" (John 8:28).

- "I have not even come on My own initiative, but He sent Me" (John 8:42).

- "I did not speak on My own initiative, but the Father Himself who sent Me has given Me commandment, what to say, and what to speak" (John 12:49).

Do you get the picture? Jesus lived as a normal man who was totally helpless apart from the divine enablement of His Father. He chose at every moment to live in total dependence on His heavenly Father.

Twenty Centuries Later

If Jesus found it necessary as a man to depend on the life of His Father to be expressed through Him, what makes us think that we can manage our own lives? Before returning to His Father, He made it clear to the disciples that they were to relate to Him in the same way that He had related to the Father. In John 15, the Lord used the metaphor of a vine and its branches to illustrate how believers would live in the days to come. He said,

> Abide in Me, and I in you. As the branch cannot bear fruit of itself, unless it abides in the vine, so neither can you, unless you abide in Me. I am the vine, you are the branches; he who abides in Me, and I in him, he bears much fruit; for *apart from Me you can do nothing* (verses 4-5, emphasis added).

The definitive issue in effective Christian living today revolves around recognizing our union with Christ. He asserts that there is nothing we can do *for* Him. In the same way that the Father expressed His life through Jesus, we are to abide in Christ, allowing Him to express His life through us. Abiding in Christ simply means living each moment totally depending on His life within us to cause us to be all that He has called us to be and to do all that He purposes for us to do. Don't make this matter of abiding complicated; it simply means that we choose to let Him do the living through us at every moment of our lives.

Jesus stated over and over again that nothing He did originated with Him. The source of His behavior was the life of the Father. He lived by the life of another Person. So it is to be in the lives of believers today. Every action of our lives is to be animated by the life of the indwelling Christ.

We are not called to do anything for Him, but to simply appropriate our union with Him.

The Word That Spoiled My Victory

For 29 years one preposition spoiled my life. It kept me from enjoying my relationship with Christ and placed me under a constant strain. I thought it was my duty to live *for* Jesus. I don't want to get hung up on semantics here, but the emphasis of the New Testament is not on living *for* Christ, but on being *in* Christ. An understanding of what it means to be *in* Christ will totally transform a person's lifestyle. In my book *Grace Walk*, I describe in detail my own pilgrimage from a lifetime of legalism to the place where I began to experience the grace walk. The grace walk is the lifestyle of a believer through whom Christ is expressing His life.

---

*The emphasis of the New Testament
is not on living for Christ,
but on being in Christ.*

The words *for Christ* and *in Christ* may represent two totally different systems of living. For most of my Christian life my idea of living *for* Jesus meant dedicating myself to doing the things that He would want me to do. I read the Bible primarily to discover principles for living a godly lifestyle. I regularly committed myself to those principles. I sometimes told people that I lived by my convictions. It was my belief that if a Christian committed himself to obeying the Word of God, he would be blessed by God. That, however, is the perfect description of a legalistic Christian lifestyle. It is an attempt to gain God's

18

gain ?
Blessing?

blessings and to make spiritual progress by what we do. It is a description of a life ruled by law, not grace.

There was a major problem I faced every time I seriously examined the Bible to see if I was measuring up to what I thought God expected of me. I always discovered other commands that I wasn't yet fully obeying. Consequently I never felt completely satisfied because I always saw how far I still had to go before I would reach the place I thought I needed to be spiritually. I was committed to godly principles and I sincerely wanted to live for Jesus. Those may sound like noble aspirations, yet in reality they are subtle deceptions. Christianity is not about doing things *for* Christ. It is being *in* Him.

Compliance Without Obedience

Christianity is not a call to live by principles or to live for Jesus. To build our lives around biblical principles sounds admirable, but it is a subtle form of legalism. Of course there is instruction in the New Testament about how we are to live. Yet these instructions are not religious laws for us to follow. They are descriptions of the many ways that Christ can live His life through us as we depend on Him. New Testament Christianity is not grounded in what we do, but in what He has already done. The Bible teaches that the One who has begun the work in us will also be the One to complete it. Paul said, "Faithful is He who calls you, *and He also will bring it to pass*" (1 Thessalonians 5:24, emphasis added). The Bible is clear: Jesus will do it, not us.

There is indeed a blessing to be enjoyed as we obey the Lord, but blessings are not experienced by simply doing what God says. Sitting at my computer one day, I opened my e-mail to find a note from my friend, Roger. "Steve, why can't I get into Canaan land?" he asked. I knew that he was referring to Canaan as a picture of the victorious Christian life. "I've come out of Egypt and as far as I know, I'm doing everything God says to do. I've given up the flesh pots of Egypt, but I'm still wandering around in circles. Help me get in!"

Can you see where Roger's problem was? He states the exact reason why he believes he should be enjoying Canaan. "I'm doing everything God says to do. I've given up the flesh pots of Egypt." Roger was experiencing the results of *compliance,* not obedience. Simply doing what God says has never brought joy to anybody's life. The source of joy is Jesus, not mere compliance to the Bible's commands.

Many people struggle with the question, "Why am I not fulfilled when I'm doing all the things that I believe God wants me to do?" It's because God's purpose is not that we should focus on doing the right things. Rather, he wants us to focus on Him. *Obedience occurs as we trust Jesus within us to fulfill the desires of His Father through us.* As Jesus does that, we will fulfill the commands of the Scriptures. On the other hand, when we simply do what the Bible instructs, that is not godly obedience. It is nothing more than *compliance.* Sometimes we can comply with Bible commands just like an unsaved person can choose at any particular moment to make the right choice instead of the wrong one. For instance, the Bible says not to steal. Even an unbeliever can live up to that standard. However, just making the right choice is not obedience. That kind of choice is nothing more than empty, lifeless compliance. It requires no divine life whatsoever.

Why Can't We Live the Christian Life?

Christian living is nothing less than an expression of Divine life through mortal man. Many Christians struggle because they fail to understand God's method by which they may experience consistent victory. Why can't they live the Christian life? The bottom line is this: God never intended for them to live it. Only one Person has ever been able to live the Christ-life. That Person is Christ Jesus Himself.

Every true believer fully understands that he did nothing to become a Christian. He simply trusted Christ. Yet many believe that they must now do something to become a victorious Christian. So they substitute *trying* in the place of *trusting*. Then they wonder why it won't work. The fact is that it will never work! No matter how sincere they may be, how hard they try, or how much they ask for God's help, they will never be able to live the Christian life. It isn't hard for them to live it; it's impossible! If you haven't seen that yet, give it time. However, I assume that you may already suspect that to be the case. For many years, I didn't know how to experience consistent victory because I didn't understand the whole story of salvation. I knew enough to get to heaven, but not enough to enjoy heaven on earth. I understood mercy, but not grace.

Meet Mercy and Grace

Every Christian understands the power of the cross as it relates to the forgiveness of sin. Because Jesus took our guilt upon Himself, incurring the wrath of God against our sin, the justice of God was satisfied (Romans 3:23-26). Our sins can be forgiven through Jesus Christ because He stood in our place when God exacted the penalty for them. When we trust Jesus Christ for the forgiveness of our sins, at that very moment God's forgiveness becomes effectual in us. We deserved to be eternally separated from God in hell, but through Jesus Christ we have received God's *mercy.* That is, we didn't receive something that we really deserve.

Some years ago when I served as a pastor in Alabama I was driving from Birmingham back to my church about an hour away. When I exited the interstate I didn't adjust my speed for the highway. In a few moments I heard a siren and saw the flashing blue lights in my rearview mirror. Glancing down at my speedometer, I thought, *Oh no! Now I've done it. I'm caught.*

The policeman walked up to my window and asked to see my driver's license. "Sir, do you know how fast you were going?" he asked. "Yes sir, I do," I answered, trying to look as "reverendly" as I knew how. "Would you please step out of the car and sit in the front seat of the squad car?" he asked in a matter-of-fact way.

I quickly walked back to his car and sat down in the front seat, cowering and hoping that none of my church members would drive by and see their pastor in the front seat of a police car. After showing me my recorded speed on his radar, the policeman reached for his ticket book. He opened it and took his pen out of his pocket. Just as he flipped open the book, I said, "Officer?" "Yes?" he responded, looking at me. "Will you give me mercy?" I asked. The policeman looked at me for a moment, looked down at his ticket book, then looked back at me. "Okay, I'll do it," he answered. "Slow down, and have a safe day."

That really happened! (Don't think that's how it always is with preachers. Another policeman who gave me a ticket said that of all people I should know better than to break the law.) Do you see what happened? I deserved the ticket, but the officer gave me a break. I didn't get what I deserved.

That's how the mercy of God is expressed toward us. We all deserve to pay the full penalty for sin (Romans 3:23). It would certainly be *just* for us to be eternally separated from Him. Yet God has chosen to extend His mercy toward us. We are like the woman who went to a photographer to have her portrait taken. After several days she returned to look at the proofs. Flipping through each one, she turned up her nose and said, "These pictures don't do me justice." "Lady," the photographer answered, "you don't need justice, you need *mercy*." That's exactly what we needed and that's exactly what God gave us when He forgave our sin.

Yet there is another aspect of the gospel that many people don't understand. Let's go back to that policeman in Alabama. Some people have said to me, "That guy really showed you grace, didn't he?" The answer to that question is no. He showed me no grace whatsoever, only mercy. However, suppose that when I started to get out of his car, the officer had said, "Wait just a minute. I'm not finished with you yet." Imagine if I had sat back down in the car as he reached into his pocket, pulled out his wallet, and handed me a $100 bill. "I want you to have this," he says. "Have a great day." Now, *that* would have been grace. (Sadly, that part of the story didn't happen.)

Mercy is not receiving something that we deserve, and grace is receiving something that we *don't* deserve. God showed us mercy when He forgave our sins and declined to hold us accountable for them. Then He went another step further and extended His grace to us, giving us divine life in the Person of Jesus Christ! Forgiveness is wonderful, but it isn't the main event. Forgiveness is the prerequisite for God's primary goal. The most wonderful thing that takes place when we are saved is that we receive the life of Jesus Christ within us.

Why Does Jesus Live Inside Us?

Have you ever stopped to consider why the Spirit of Jesus comes into us at salvation? Jesus told His disciples that after He left this earth physically, His Spirit would come and live inside believers forever (John 14:16-17). We often speak of being saved in terms of Jesus coming into us. Why is that necessary? Consider some of the common misconceptions about why He comes into us at salvation.

• *Jesus comes into us so that our sins can be forgiven.* It's not necessary for Jesus to come into us so that our sins can be forgiven. Couldn't God have forgiven us without placing His life within us? Yes, His mercy would have taken care of that without the grace of having Christ indwell us.

• *He comes into us so that we can go to heaven.* Did Jesus come into us so that we could go to heaven? Why would it be necessary for Him to come into us on this earth just for that reason? He could take us to heaven without placing His life within us.

• *Jesus comes into us so that we will know how to live.* Is He inside us so that we can know what to do in life? No, because the Bible tells us the mind of God concerning how we are to live in this world. It isn't necessary for Christ to come into us for that reason.

There is one simple reason why the Spirit of Jesus Christ comes into us at salvation. It is so that we can experience and express His life. Jesus clearly said He came so that we might have *life* (John 10:10). Before we were saved, we were spiritually dead, but now we are alive (Ephesians 2:1). The fundamental characteristic of the Christian's life is that Jesus has given His life to us and desires to express it through us at every moment. Christian living is not *me* serving Jesus. It is not *me* living for Him. It is not *me* doing the things that God instructs me to do. The Christian life is *Him*! This grace walk is nothing less than the Christ-life. It is New Testament Christianity. It is Christ *being* Christ in us and through us at every moment.

For 29 years of my Christian life, I diligently tried to live for Jesus. Although I was saved, law (religious rules) ruled my life. What a wonderful discovery it was when I realized that I couldn't live for Him. In fact, my trying to live for Him actually interfered with His purposes!

God doesn't need us to live for Him. He will live through us as we live in absolute dependence on Him at each moment. This is exactly what it means to allow grace to rule our life. However before we can do that, there is a fundamental truth we must understand. This truth makes all the difference in whether we experience victory or defeat.

Walking Together

Let's walk together with the Holy Spirit through this book. As God reveals truth to you, it will be helpful to participate with Him at each step where He works in your life. If the prayers at the end of each chapter express your heart, then affirm to God that they reflect your thoughts and desires. You will get more out of this book if you pause at the end of each chapter and interact with your heavenly Father.

· · ·

Dear Father,

   I have experienced a struggle in my life as I've tried to serve You. I see that at times I have focused more on my own behavior than on Jesus. I now understand that I'm not supposed to try to live for You, but instead I am to allow You to live Your life through me. Teach me how to experience obedience motivated by love instead of duty. I can't live the Christian life in my own power; show me how You can live Your life through me!

Help me to understand how to obey your word, but not be legalistic. Father when I do not walk in accordence with your word I feel conviction. Is that not your Sprit within me? You know I am struggling with "apropriate" entertainment. Is that legalistic? Help me to understand. Oh please forgive me if what has happened b/w Sarah & I was wrong. I made my choice based upon your word and a conviction in my heart. Truly I believe I am to live in accordence with your entiere word. That means obeying the law. Of course I compleltly need you in order to do so. I need you to rule over me, to teach me, direct me and help me live. If there is a problem in my beliefs, my truth — show me, change me. My life is yours, do with it your will. In my saviors name — Amen.

G.R.A.C.E. Group Questions

A G.R.A.C.E. (Giving & Receiving Affirmative Christian Encouragement) Group is any group of people who gather together in order to encourage and strengthen each other in the grace of God. At the end of each chapter are discussion questions to help facilitate further learning and discussion. The truths of this book will be worked further into your life as you consider these questions.

1. Read Acts 17:25. What is your opinion of the idea that God doesn't need us to serve Him? What difference will it makc in a person's perspective if he believes that God *needs* him as opposed to the idea that God *wants* him?

2. The "kenosis" theory suggests that Jesus emptied Himself of divine prerogatives. Explain the importance of the theory in view of John 5:19. What difference would it make if the lifestyle of Jesus had been sustained by His divine nature?

3. List five differences between living *for* Christ and living *in* Christ.

4. What is the difference between compliance and obedience?

5. Define *mercy* and *grace*. What is the difference between the two? What is the result of experiencing God's mercy? What is the result of experiencing His grace?

6. Read John 14:16-17. Why does the Holy Spirit come into a person when he trusts Christ for salvation? How can trying to live for Jesus out of our own strength cause problems in life?

2

The Liability of Ability

*T*HE MAN FELT a surge of anger at the sight of his brother being mercilessly beaten by a brutal bully. This one he loved lay crumpled in the dirt with his hands over his head, trying to protect himself from the attack. Having beaten him to the ground, the attacker now kicked him in the side as his victim groaned in agony. Sensing that he must act quickly, the man instinctively moved forward toward the attacker and his victim. Looking around as he advanced, he saw that there was no one else in sight—just this evil bully, his helpless victim, and himself. Coming up from behind, he struck the assailant hard on the back of his head. Very hard. The bully staggered backward, trying to keep his balance. The man drew back and, with all his strength, struck him again. The assailant fell to the ground. He didn't make a sound. He wasn't breathing. Blood began to ooze out of his nose and ears. It was obvious—he was dead.

The victim, surprised at this turn of events, looked at his attacker for a moment, then looked up at his rescuer.

He didn't say a word, but quickly turned and ran. In spite of his injuries, he ran fast. The man watched him disappear into a nearby building, then looked around again. He still saw no one. Quickly he picked up the corpse from the ground and ran. He knew he had to dispose of the body before anyone knew what he had done. He felt justified in what had happened, but knew that the authorities wouldn't understand.

Only one person had witnessed what he had done. Just one. Yet because of that one eyewitness—the victim no less—he was to become a fugitive from the law. For 40 years he would go into hiding.

A PG-Rated Story in a G-Rated Book

Does this story sound like a movie preview you have seen? It's a story about treason and murder and a fleeing felon. However, the scene didn't come from a movie script. It came from a book. It is found in the Bible in Exodus chapter 2. The rescuer who became a fugitive was Moses. He is mentioned in Hebrews 11 as a man of great faith, but he didn't start out that way. We are told in Exodus 2:11 that Moses had grown up, and then in the very next verse we read that he murdered someone. Not exactly the kind of beginning you would expect in the life of a man who would ultimately become one of the greatest men of God who ever lived!

Among the men of the Bible whose lives had a major impact on this world, none offer more hope for the average man than Moses. Although he lived millenniums before the cross, his life reflects the grace-filled manner in which God prepares those whom He intends to use for His own glory. Unless you have done something as horrible as Moses did, you're already one step ahead of Moses in the journey toward a fulfilling and distinguished life. And even if you have erred grievously, you're no further from God's plan than Moses was at the beginning of his adulthood.

Josh came to me one day, obviously discouraged. "Steve, I don't know what my problem is. Maybe I've done too many wrong things for God to ever be able to use me. I can't seem to experience victory in my Christian life no matter how hard I try." I knew his background. He had made some serious mistakes in judgment, even after he was saved. Now he was convinced that his sins disqualified him from being useful to God.

Moses was motivated by a God-given desire, but he made one fatal mistake. He acted out of his own ability.

Have you ever felt like that? When we try to understand why we aren't experiencing fulfillment in life, we always look in the wrong place to find answers. Josh believed that it was his moral weakness which prevented him from finding real joy in life. Yet his weakness wasn't the problem at all. If God only used sinless people, every one of us would have to sit on the sidelines. Many Christians believe that we need to be strong if God is going to use our lives. The reality, however, is that we don't become strong enough for God to use. Instead, we must become *weak* enough. We may think we need to dedicate our abilities to God, asking Him to help us to use them for His glory. While that sounds admirable, it is actually the surest way to experience continual defeat. Josh had to discover that he wasn't too weak to be used by God. He was too strong. His motive was right, but his method for living the Christian life was all wrong.

Right Motive, Wrong Method

Moses certainly was motivated by a proper desire. All his life he had identified inwardly with his own people. Seeing an Egyptian taskmaster beating his Jewish brother deeply stirred his compassion. Moses sensed deep within himself a desire to free the people of Israel. It was within his nature to deliver the Jews from Egyptian oppression. God had placed into him a calling. He saw a need and wanted to do something about it. He was motivated by a God-given desire, but he made one fatal mistake: He acted out of his own ability. Depending on his strength, he moved forward to do what he perceived would be the right thing. However, he was to discover that trying to do something godly out of his own strength would ultimately lead to major defeat.

Every person who has been born again has an inner desire to glorify God in his behavior. We want to be used by Him. That desire is a part of our nature. For almost three decades of my Christian life, I fell into the same trap as Moses. I sensed an inward desire for my life to make a difference in this world. So I dedicated myself to God and sought to use my ability for His glory. Like Moses, my motive was right. However, my method was totally wrong. God never asks us to use our ability to do anything for Him. His plan is that we rely totally on His ability, not ours. It is not by our might or power that His work is accomplished, but rather it is by the power of His Spirit within us. Many Christians live in defeat and frustration because they can't experience victory in spite of all their godly desires and good intentions. The problem is not their motive, but their method of living. When we live out of our own self-sufficiency, law rules. It is important to remember that a primary characteristic of a legalistic lifestyle is the emphasis on what *I* do. When grace rules, we live by an entirely different method.

The prescribed method for our lifestyle is clearly set forth in the book of Acts when Peter preached on the day of Pentecost. In speaking of Jesus, Peter plainly tells how He lived:

> Men of Israel, listen to these words: Jesus the Nazarene, a man attested to you by God with miracles and wonders and signs which *God performed through Him* in your midst... (Acts 2:22, emphasis added).

The Bible says it was God who performed the miracles, wonders, and signs Jesus did. Our Lord did not live out of His own ability. He lived out of the infinite ability of His Father. Peter stressed that Jesus was a man who relied on His Father to accomplish His work. If Jesus chose to depend totally on His Father to empower His life and actions, what makes us think that we can do anything for God by our own natural abilities?

The Seminary of Suffering

Moses' desire to help his people was so great that he took matters into his own hands and ended up murdering an Egyptian. He still had much to learn about God's methods. He didn't know it, but God was making plans for him to enroll in seminary so that he could learn God's way of doing things.

The day after Moses killed the Egyptian, he went out and saw two Hebrews fighting with each other. He rushed over to them and asked one of them, "Why are you striking your companion?" One of the men asked him, "Who made you a prince or judge over us? Are you intending to kill me, like you did the Egyptian?" Moses' blood ran cold within him. He realized word had gotten out. Just as he feared, Pharaoh heard about the incident and tried to kill him. So Moses ran, narrowly escaping into the desert of Midian. Little did he know that his sovereign God was waiting in the desert, where He was going to teach Moses a truth that would totally transform his life.

> *God loves you so much that He will use pain if necessary to bring you into a dependent relationship with Him.*

How quickly the events of life can change! One day Moses lives in the courts of Pharaoh; the next day he is living in the desert. He no longer smells the fragrant perfume of royal beauties, but instead the stench of stinking sheep fills his nostrils. No linen sheets cover his bed tonight. He sleeps on a bed of straw under the stars. He has exchanged the robes of royalty for the tattered tunic of a shepherd. Everything is gone. It's all lost. He was a prince, but now he is a lowly shepherd. Why would God allow this to happen to a man whose only desire was to deliver a godly people from wicked oppressors?

In 1989 I felt that I was a successful pastor. I was serving a growing church. I received constant affirmation and recognition. In all the ways that I measured success back then, I felt good. Then God took me to a place where all that changed. All the things that had worked for me in the past didn't work anymore. In fact, nothing I did worked. I blamed myself. I blamed my church. I even blamed God. Over a period of time, God began to teach me what He took Moses to the wilderness to learn. God doesn't want us to trust in our own ability. Like Moses, many of us must discover this the hard way. We usually learn it living in a dry and barren place.

Don't believe the lie that God has forgotten you when you find yourself living in difficult circumstances. God has a reason for your being there. Don't give Satan the glory for your troubles! God is sovereign over the enemy and He will use your pain to accomplish His purposes. God will use the desert experiences of life to shake away from us everything except Himself. The lie may flood your mind that God doesn't care about what is happening to you, but He does! He loves you so much that He will use pain if necessary to bring you into a dependent relationship with Him.

When my son, David, was about three years old, he woke up one night crying in agony. Melanie and I rushed into his bedroom and could immediately tell that something was seriously wrong. We agreed that she would stay at home with the other children and I would take him to the hospital. When we arrived at the emergency room, the attending physician examined him. He turned to me and said, "I know your son's problem. He has an intestinal blockage that must be cleared. Neither his bladder nor bowels have emptied in a long time. For that reason, David is experiencing intense pain." "What has to be done?" I asked. "Two things," the doctor answered. "First, it will be necessary to catheterize him." I shuddered at the thought. "Then," he added "we must administer a barium enema."

After assuring me that there were no other treatment options, I set David down on the examining table. When the doctor began the procedure with the catheter, David started to come up off the table. "You'll have to hold him down," the doctor instructed. Leaning across the body of my three-year-old son, I placed my right arm over his left shoulder and my left arm over his right shoulder so that he couldn't move. David began to cry, hysterically screaming, "Daddy, make him stop! Daddy, please! Make him stop! Make him stop!" Then there was that moment—sort of like suspended animation—one of those freeze-frame moments that you never forget as long as you live. David stopped crying, looked deeply into my eyes, and with obvious terror and confusion asked, "Daddy, *why* won't you make him stop?"

How do you explain a catheter to a three-year-old? How could I get his young mind to understand the valid reason for such pain? I couldn't answer because he wouldn't have understood. I began to cry too. I laid myself down across him and hugged him close to me and to the table. "It's okay, son. Daddy's here with you. You must trust me, David. This is necessary. It's for your good. I'll hold you until it's over."

I can remember times in my own life when I have cried out to my heavenly Father, "Make it stop! Make it stop! *Why* won't you make it stop?" Have you been there? Maybe you are at that place in life right now. Your circumstances don't seem to make sense. It may appear that God has abandoned you, but He hasn't. He may be holding you on the table so that you can't get up, but *He is hugging you!* He takes no pleasure in your pain, yet He loves you enough that if it takes pain to bring you to the place where He can accomplish His purpose for your good, He will allow it and keep you in it as long as necessary. Be assured that He won't keep you on the table a minute longer than necessary.

The Poison of Self-Sufficiency

God had plans for Moses in the wilderness. The first 40 years of his life had been majestic. The last 40 years would be miraculous as he led the people out of Egypt. However, these middle 40 years were going to be miserable. God was bringing Moses to the end of himself and his confidence in his abilities so that he might know and rest in the ability of God.

Moses, of course, was most likely confused. He had gone from being a prince to being a shepherd. That wasn't exactly the way he had thought things would turn out. After a while, he probably figured that he would be living the rest of his life in quiet obscurity. But then came the burning bush.

In Exodus 3–4, the account is told of Moses' encounter with God. God reveals to him that He plans to use him to deliver the Hebrews from bondage. Yet because of his circumstances, Moses had probably developed some serious doubts about his ability as a leader. He may have thought that because he was a shepherd tending to sheep, he had lost his people skills. He may have reasoned, "The only ability that I can count on any more is my skill as a shepherd."

Then God spoke:

> "What is that in your hand?" And he said, "A staff." Then He said, "Throw it on the ground."

So he threw it on the ground, and it became a
serpent; and Moses fled from it (Exodus 4:2,3).

Have you ever felt that God has taken everything that
He can take, and then He finds something else to take
away from you? That's where Moses was in this passage.
The staff was a symbol of Moses' ability as a shepherd. It
wasn't much, but at least he was surviving through his
ability to herd sheep.

Notice what God says about the staff, which represents the ability in which Moses was still trusting: "Throw
it down." When Moses threw the staff to the ground, it
became a serpent. Finally Moses saw what God wanted
him to see. He still had not come to the end of himself. He
had simply exchanged his abilities as a prince for his abilities as a shepherd. Both types of ability were simply two
different ways of managing his own life. Now he saw it for
what it is. The very ability that he had been trusting had
been poisonous to him all along and he hadn't even
known it!

Mike began to talk to me one day about his frustration. "Steve, I don't get it. Before I was saved, I partied. I
drank too much, made immoral choices, and even exper-
imented with drugs. When I became a Christian I turned
my back on all that. I'm involved in my church now. I
teach a boy's Sunday school class. I sing in the choir. I try
to be available to the pastor anytime he needs someone to
do something." As we talked further, I finally suggested
what I believed his problem to be.

"Mike, it sounds to me like you used to meet your
need for fulfillment in the wrong ways." "I did," he
answered. "Have you ever considered that you might still
be trying to find fulfillment in the wrong way?" I asked.
Mike look puzzled, so I continued. "It seems that perhaps

you have simply traded a bad identity for a better identity. You don't see yourself as a party animal anymore. Now you see yourself as a church worker." "So what's wrong with working in the church?" he asked. "Nothing is wrong with working in church. It's a good thing. However, God didn't plan for us to find fulfillment in *good things*. He desires that we be fulfilled in *Him*." As we continued to talk, Mike began to see the problem. Although he wasn't relying on his old identity to get his needs met, he was still relying on his abilities and not Christ.

Ability becomes a liability when we trust in the ability instead of trusting in God.

Moses had exchanged a royal life for a shepherd's life, but had not yet experienced God's life! Moses was thinking that the only ability he could count on anymore was his ability as a shepherd, but God was showing him that he couldn't even depend on that. We can only experience the life of God when we throw down our life. Jesus said in Matthew 16:25, "Whoever wishes to save his life shall lose it; but whoever loses his life for My sake shall find it." We experience God's life only when we renounce our own ability to manage life.

Harvey sat down across from me. "I don't understand my life, Steve. I am a successful businessman. I have a good marriage. My kids are well behaved. Our financial circumstances are secure. Yet I can't seem to live a victorious Christian life. Why am I able to succeed in so many areas and still be an utter failure in the most important area of my life?"

"Do you want my honest opinion?" I asked him.

"Of course," he answered.

"Harvey, I think you're too sharp for your own good. You've achieved success in the other major areas of your life and people admire you for it. You are an achiever, there's no doubt about it."

"Then what's the problem?" he interrupted.

"The problem is that you can't *achieve* victory in the Christian life. You can only *receive* it." Harvey made a mistake which is common to many believers. A victorious life isn't the result of trying, but instead comes from trusting Jesus Christ to express His life through us. We must renounce confidence in our ability, acknowledging that it is only by His indwelling life that we can accomplish anything of value. I'm not saying there is anything wrong with natural ability; it is God who has given us every ability we possess. However, we must recognize the inherent danger that comes with ability. *Ability becomes a liability when we trust in the ability instead of trusting in God.*

Moses looked at the serpent representing his ability and saw that fact. He was repulsed by how he had trusted in himself at all. He wanted nothing to do with it ever again. The Bible says that he "fled from it." Yet it wasn't the ability itself which was wrong, it was the feeling of self-sufficiency that he had allowed into his life. He never wanted to live that way again.

Ability Animated by God

Now that Moses saw the folly of trusting in himself, it was safe for him to again take up his abilities. That's why God told him to "'stretch out your hand and grasp it by its tail'—so he stretched out his hand and caught it and it became a staff in his hand" (Exodus 4:4). Picking up the serpent by the tail made Moses very aware of his vulnerability toward what he held in his hand. The only way he could ensure that he wouldn't be infected with its venom was if he continually trusted the Lord to protect him from it. Likewise, none of us ever reach the place where we become immune to the venom of the self-life. The staff we hold always has the potential of becoming a poisonous serpent in our hands. We must abide in Christ moment by moment, realizing that without His empowering presence the serpent of self-sufficiency will strike us, infecting us with its poison.

Once we have seen the error of placing our confidence in our abilities, we are at a place where we can be trusted with them. God will then allow us to pick them up again, depending on Him to animate that same ability by His power. Before coming to that realization our abilities are empowered by self-determination; afterward, they are animated by the very life of Jesus Christ.

When God first asked Moses what he held in his hand, he answered, "A staff." Yet in Exodus 4:20, when Moses is preparing to leave the desert and go back to Egypt where he will fulfill his calling, the Bible says that "Moses also took the staff of God in his hand." From that point forward in Scripture it was never called "the staff," but rather "the staff of God." Once God has brought us to the end of self-confidence, others may not see the change that has taken place in our attitude toward natural ability, but we know. To others it's the same old stick, but within our heart we know that our natural ability has been transformed into supernatural ability by His life within us.

When God brought me to the end of myself in 1990, He caused me to be repulsed by how I had trusted in my own ability. Like Moses, I wanted to run. When the day came that I began to learn about trusting in His supernatural ability and not my own, the difference was like day and night. I'll never forget the first time I saw what God could do if I would trust Him instead of myself.

When Miracles Happen

Phillipe knocked on the door of my office. He introduced himself to me and we began to discuss why he was in Atlanta. I discovered that he was from Cameroon and that he had come to Georgia to study hospital administration. As we talked, it became apparent that Phillipe was not a Christian. During that first visit together I was able to share the gospel with him and he received Jesus Christ and was born again. We agreed that he would come back each Tuesday morning and I would teach him from the Bible how to live the Christian life.

A Christian will see the miraculous work of God in and through him to the extent that he renounces self-sufficiency and rests in the all-sufficient Holy Spirit within him.

Every week he came to my office and for two hours I shared with him from Scripture about what it means to be a Christian. We talked about who he was in Christ and about what it means to abide in Jesus. We studied how to allow Jesus to live His life through us. I was happy to see the spiritual growth he was experiencing as he became more grounded in Christ.

After about six weeks he paused before leaving at the end of our time together. "Steve, have you noticed that I always take notes when we study together?" he asked. "Yes, I have," I answered. "Do you know why I take extensive notes while you are teaching me?" he continued. "Phillipe, I assume that you take the notes back to your apartment and study them during the following week," I answered.

"No, that's not it," he said. "You see, each week I write everything you say, translating it into my native language. Then when I leave here, I place the notes into a package and immediately go to the post office where I mail the package to the chief of my village at home. Every week when he receives the notes, he goes outside his hut and calls the people of my village together. Then he teaches them from the notes all the things that you have taught me. Some of the people of my village are being saved and are asking him questions. He doesn't know the answers, so he writes and asks me, but I don't know the answers either. I told him that I would ask you if you would be willing to answer their questions if I translate for you."

Suddenly it hit me. I thought of all the years I had tried to produce something spiritual; all the time that I had spent trying to make a difference. I had sincerely used my abilities for God, but always felt frustrated. Now here was God doing it Himself. I was meeting with one man in Atlanta and I was also evangelizing and discipling a whole village of people in Africa! Only God can do that!

A miracle is an act of God which defies natural explanation. Do you know when miracles happen? A Christian will see the miraculous work of God in and through him to the extent that he renounces self-sufficiency and rests in the all-sufficient Holy Spirit within him. When Moses left the desert, having recognized the foolishness of trusting in his own ability, he returned to Egypt expecting miracles as the norm of life. God told him that he would "perform before Pharaoh all the wonders which I have put in your power" (Exodus 4:21). A man who has been broken of confidence in himself yet has absolute confidence in God is one who can be entrusted with power to perform wonders. When grace rules, miracles happen!

When Peter and John met the lame man at the gate of the temple in Jerusalem, Peter took the man's hand and told him to get up and walk. The man, who had been lame from the day of his birth, began to walk, then run, and finally leap for joy. The crowd pressed in around Peter, amazed by his ability to perform such a feat. They thought Peter had impressive power. Yet Peter knew the truth. He had learned about his own ability on the night he failed to stand for Jesus after promising that he would die for him if necessary. He quickly answered the crowd, "Why do you marvel at this, or why do you gaze at us, as if by our own power or piety we had made him walk?" (Acts 3:12). He then immediately pointed them to Jesus as the cause of what they had witnessed.

Peter saw the ability of the Lord functioning through him. So did Moses. Why would any Christian today settle for what human ability can accomplish when we have the opportunity to experience the supernatural results of God's ability? God has prepared something great for every Christian. Willingness to renounce confidence in our own abilities is a vital step in preparation for receiving the recipe for experiencing the outflow of God's divine life— a recipe we'll look at in the next chapter.

• • •

Dear Father,

I see it now. The problem hasn't been that I haven't had the desire to glorify You. I've been going about trying to live the Christian life the wrong way. All this time that I've been asking You to help me to live for You, I have thought that You would bless my ability to live the Christian life. Now I see that this will never work. Right now I willingly lay down my ability. My confidence in it has poisoned my life. I never want to trust in my ability again. I trust only You, Lord Jesus. Teach me how to experience Your ability.

G.R.A.C.E. Group Questions

1. Read Exodus 2:11-15. How did Moses initially depend on his own ability to deliver Israel from Egyptian bondage? Discuss ways that modern congregations sometimes depend on natural ability to facilitate church ministry.

2. What would you tell a Christian who is experiencing prolonged suffering and wonders why God won't bring it to an end? How do you answer the argument that God doesn't want his children to hurt? What was the purpose for Moses' wilderness years?

3. Steve described the circumstances of Mike, a person who had found fulfillment from partying, alcohol, and illicit sex before he was saved. He was frustrated because now that he was a Christian, he served the Lord faithfully yet still felt unfulfilled. What was his problem? Why do you think that many sincere Christians in the church today aren't fulfilled in life?

4. What would you tell someone who says, "I tried the Christian life and it just doesn't work for me."?

5. Describe the difference between living from natural ability and supernatural ability.

6. Read Acts 3:1-12. How was Peter able to make a lame man walk? Based on what you learned about Moses and Peter, what would be required for your church to see God work in the same ways?

3

The Nectar of Heaven

*I*NGREDIENTS:
   2 Family-Size Tea Bags
   1 Gallon Water
   2 Cups White Sugar

Place the tea bags in a small simmering pan containing about two cups of water. Bring to a boil.

Steep for ten minutes, then pour tea concentrate into gallon pitcher.

While liquid is still very hot, add two cups of sugar. Stir.

Fill gallon pitcher with water and stir.

Serve over ice.

On behalf of everybody who grew up in the southern United States, I proudly present to you the recipe for Sweet Tea. I have found as I travel that in many parts of the United States and especially abroad, people have been culturally deprived of this delight all of their lives. Try asking a waitress in Pittsburgh for sweet tea. She points at the sugar on the table and then looks at you like you must be blind or something. It's sad; she just doesn't get it. As I write these words, I am in Canada. In the spirit of good international relations, we won't even talk about the tea in restaurants here. Have you ever watched a person drink Earl Grey tea over a few pieces of ice with no sugar? It's not a pretty sight. And Mexico? The tea there brings to mind the age-old question, "How can a loving God allow such suffering?" Since this is the beverage that will probably be served at the Marriage Feast of the Lamb, we would all be well advised to learn to enjoy it now! In Georgia, we think of it as the nectar of heaven.

Seriously, why have I shared the recipe for sweet tea with you? Well, putting aside the obvious culinary mission of mercy, it actually illustrates very clearly some truths about what happens in a person's life when grace rules. God's recipe for transforming us by His grace given in Christ has some striking similarities to the recipe at the beginning of this chapter.

A Recipe for Transformation

Turn Up the Heat

The first step in making sweet tea is to turn up the heat so that the water will boil. The sugar and tea won't permeate the water unless it is very hot. This is the same way that God works in a person when He is preparing to make something wonderful of his life. Have you ever noticed how much more receptive you are to God when the heat is turned up high in your life? When you are in hot water, you usually get into the receiving mode fast! If you have ever asked God to use your life, then don't be surprised when trouble comes. God may turn up the heat in your circumstances to prepare you to experience His life. The glory of having Jesus expressing His life through you requires that you pass through the fire. It's not pleasant while it is happening, but when the process is complete the finished product is quite a treat!

The Apostle Peter said:

> Beloved, do not be surprised at the fiery ordeal among you, which comes upon you for your testing, as though some strange thing were happening to you; but to the degree that you share the sufferings of Christ, keep on rejoicing; so that also at the revelation of His glory, you may rejoice with exultation (1 Peter 4:12-13).

The fire may be hot, but don't despair in your troubles. God often orchestrates the events of our lives to bring us to the end of confidence in our own ability so that He may readily complete His recipe for godliness within us. "The revelation of His glory" that Peter mentions is not a reference to heaven, but to the discovery of the sweet truth of our union with Christ. However, it is impossible to make sweet tea without hot water.

Add the Sugar and Stir

Unlike cold tea, hot tea and sugar are totally compatible with each other. In fact, the sugar quickly dissolves when stirred into the hot tea. Once the sugar has dissolved into the water, the very nature of the liquid is changed. The tea and sugar can never be separated again. Their distinct elements have merged together in such a way that they are now one new entity. This isn't the case with iced tea. It is impossible to get sugar to dissolve in tea once it has been served over ice. No matter how much you stir it, the two just won't mix.

When God prepares to manifest the sweet presence of His life within us, He uses heat to cause us to be compatible with Him permeating our being. It's when He turns up the heat that He will often allow us to experience difficulties. Then we don't resist like we would when we are spiritually cold. Once he places His life into us, our very nature is changed. Just as the sugar and tea have become one, we have been united with Him and can never again be separated from Him. First Corinthians 6:17 says, "The one who joins himself to the Lord is one spirit with Him." There is no longer my life and Christ's life. Jesus has come into me and changed my very nature so that I may say quite literally that Christ *is* my life.

I was teaching this truth in a Grace Walk Conference once and a man whose field of study was chemistry said, "It is a fact that tea has its own distinct chemical composition and sugar has its own unique chemical composition, but when you put the two together in the way you have described, a totally new chemical composition is created which is neither tea nor sugar." Do you know what it is called? Sweet tea!

The Bible says, "If any man is in Christ, he is a new creature; the old things passed away; behold, new things have come" (2 Corinthians 5:17). When we received Christ, we gained a brand new identity. When have you ever heard someone refer to tea as "water with tea and sugar in it"? Its nature has been changed; therefore, it is identified by its new identity—sweet tea.

Fill the Pitcher with Water

Once the sugar has been placed into the tea, the pitcher must be filled with water. Then the tea is ready to be shared with others. In the Bible, water is a type of the Holy Spirit. The Bible says that the treasure of the life of Jesus is contained in the earthen vessels of our bodies (2 Corinthians 4:7). Yet we must be filled with the Holy Spirit if people are going to be attracted to Christ within us (Ephesians 5:18). To be filled with the Holy Spirit means nothing less than Jesus Christ consuming our total being and expressing His life through us.

It is the *Holy* Spirit who dwells within our spirit. That same Spirit is the very spirit of Jesus. Since He has come to us, our nature has changed. We now possess the nature of God. By the death and resurrection of Jesus, God works in this world to create a new race of people who possess His nature. Second Peter 1:4 says that through the Spirit of Christ we have "become partakers of the divine nature." Our new nature is a holy nature.

Tea with Sugar Just Isn't the Same

I enjoy sweet tea, but I don't like tea with sugar in it. Some may ask, "Isn't it the same thing?" Not at all. When I'm traveling, I sometimes order iced tea and put sugar in it, but the tea never gets sweet enough for my taste. I sometimes have a glass of iced tea on the table with half an inch of sugar settled at the bottom of the glass. That is tea with sugar, but it's not sweet tea. It is only when the sugar has dissolved in the tea that it receives a sweet nature.

Similarly, there's a difference between Christ merely being in my life and Christ *being* my life. When we were saved, Jesus didn't simply come into our life. The Bible teaches that He has so filled our being that He *is* our life. The very essence of our being has been changed through this supernatural union with Him.

If I held up a glass and declared it to be full of sweet tea, someone might argue that it isn't the tea which is sweet, but it's the sugar in the tea that is sweet. I would disagree. The sugar has so diffused its life into the tea that the nature of the tea has changed. Yes, the tea is sweet.

> *God has already made you holy.*
> *You don't have to try to be holy*
> *in order to become holy.*
> *You already are.*
> *We desire to live holy lives*
> *because He has made us holy.*

The Bible teaches that because Christ has come into us, we have been made righteous. Some may argue that it isn't we who are righteous, but rather it is only Jesus within us who is righteous. This is a mistake. We have been made righteous by the presence of His life within us. We have a brand new nature—a righteous one! Paul said, "He made Him who knew no sin to be sin on our behalf, that we might become the righteousness of God in Him" (2 Corinthians 5:21). If a person perceives his own identity only in terms of Jesus being present in his life, he will fail to understand the radical transformation which took place at salvation. God didn't improve your life at salvation; He created a brand new person—one like Jesus!

Many Christians fail, however, to understand the reality of the righteousness which becomes ours when we enter into Christ. Because they don't *feel* righteous, they interpret what the Bible says about the matter in a way that falls short of the truth. It is vital for a Christian to recognize that God took away the unrighteousness he possessed before being saved. Believers have been given the righteous nature of Jesus. Those who fail to understand this gift are doomed to a legalistic lifestyle, always trying to achieve righteousness by their works. Grace is the means by which God *gives* us righteousness. It is not something we achieve, but rather something that we receive in Christ. Romans 5:17 says that when we experienced the abundance of grace we also received the *gift* of righteousness.

Hal was witnessing to his friend Ray one day when Ray told him, "I'm really trying to be a Christian." Hal responded, "Ray, you can't *try* to become a Christian. You can only trust Jesus, believing what God says about how a person receives eternal life through him." Did Hal give an appropriate response to Ray? Of course he did. Yet consider the following remark made by Ray after he became a Christian. "Hal, since I have been saved I really want to be righteous. I want you to pray for me because I'm trying to be holy so that God will be glorified." How should Hal respond to Ray? Many Christians would tell Ray that they will be praying for him. They might even tell him a few things to do to become more holy. Is that an appropriate response? No, it isn't. Ray needs to understand that he is *already* righteous because he has received Christ.

We could say, "Ray, when you received the life of Jesus Christ some wonderful things took place. First, you were given eternal life through Jesus. In fact, He *is* your life. Yet there's more good news than that. He has already made you holy. You don't have to try to be holy in order to become holy. You already are. We desire to live holy lives because He has made us holy. Just as Jesus has become your life, He has also become your righteousness."

The Bible Teaches That We Are Holy

The Bible teaches that we are already holy. It doesn't happen gradually. We may not feel holy or even act holy, but the ultimate authority isn't our own feelings or experiences. The final authority for the Christian is the Bible. Consider what God says about the matter in 1 Corinthians 3:16-17:

> Do you not know that you are a temple of God, and that the Spirit of God dwells in you? If any man destroy the temple of God, God will destroy Him, for the temple of God is holy, and *that is what you are*" (emphasis added).

The Bible presents an irrefutable case in the verse in three simple points. Point one: The Christian is the temple in which God now lives. Point two: The temple where God lives is holy. Point three: You are holy! Either we can believe it or we might as well take a black marker and mark through this verse in our Bible!

Paul said in Ephesians 4:24 that a Christian is a person "which in the likeness of God has been created in righteousness and holiness of the truth." I'll state it again for emphasis: Righteousness is not something that we gain by living a certain way. When law rules, the focus is on what *we* do. Grace always centers on what *God* has done through Jesus Christ.

Is Our Righteousness Only Positional?

For years I couldn't reconcile what I saw taught in the Bible about the Christian's righteousness with my understanding of my own experience. I read verses like those already mentioned, but struggled with my own inconsistent behavior. So I took this aspect of truth to be only a positional truth. My argument went like this: "We aren't literally righteous. God only sees us that way. Our position is one of righteousness, but our condition is that we are unrighteous." Let's dissect that argument for a moment. We'll get rid of the glaring error first—the idea that God only sees us as righteous. Exactly what could this mean? Would one suggest that God sees something that isn't really there? It reminds me of the arrogant professor who saw the unlearned custodian reading his Bible and sneered, "Do you believe that book as it is?" Without hesitation, the custodian replied, "Do you believe it as it ain't?" That's a good question for this matter. Does God see something as it *is* or as it *ain't*?

 Romans 5:19 corrects the error of believing that we are only positionally righteous; If we were literally sinners then, we are literally righteous now.

When we consider the argument that the righteousness of the Christian is positional but not literal we must be intellectually honest. Romans 5:19 corrects the error of believing that we are only positionally righteous:

> For as through the one man's disobedience
> the many were made sinners, even so through

the obedience of the One the many will be made righteous.

This verse very simply presents the truth of our present righteousness in Christ. Paul reminds us that in Adam we all were made to be sinners. In the same way, he says, we are made righteous in Christ. According to the principles of biblical hermeneutics, we must be consistent in interpreting Scripture. If the last half of this verse means that we are only positionally righteous in Christ, then the first part of the verse must be interpreted to say that we are only positionally sinners in Adam. Were we literally a sinner in Adam or was it only positional? If we were literally sinners then, we are literally righteous now.

Some say that the verse teaches that we will be made righteous when we get to heaven. Does that mean that a person doesn't become a sinner until he gets to hell? A man is a sinner for one simple reason—he was born in Adam. People become righteous by the same means— birth. When we are born again, we become righteous because of being placed into Christ.

Let's don't resist the truth! God says we are righteous because we are in Christ. It is a literal truth. That doesn't mean we always act that way. How we act and who we are may not always coincide. Sometimes I act like a child even though I was born in 1954. Identity isn't determined by our behavior, but by our birth. Occasionally my wife, Melanie, has even called me a big baby. But I know it's not true! I have my birth certificate to prove it!

Tea Comes in Many Flavors

Melanie often buys a brand of tea called Celestial Seasonings.™ The package contains tea bags of different flavors.

She likes the Country Apple flavor. I don't care for it, but I do enjoy a flavor called Red Zinger. The apple flavor is boring to me, but the Red Zinger—it's a real eye-opener. When a person is thirsty for some good tea, Red Zinger hits the spot. Melanie disagrees. She thinks the Country Apple is better. However, it isn't the actual flavor of either tea that quenches our thirst. As much as we each enjoy our favorite flavors, we have never taken the tea bags out of the box and put them into our mouth to suck the flavor out of the bags. We always add water. The flavor causes the tea to appeal to us, but the water is what really satisfies.

Jesus once said, "If any man is thirsty, let him come to Me and drink" (John 7:37). Only Jesus can quench the inner thirst for life experienced by every human being. Jesus offers Himself as the only real thirst quencher in this barren world. The way in which He offers His life to the world is ingenious. His life is expressed through many different flavors.

Just as there are many flavors of tea, there is amazing diversity within the body of Christ. There are distinct differences which are obvious. I've met some Country Apples in the body of Christ more than once. I have often seen the distinguished Earl Grey crowd. I have even met a few Red Zingers along the way. Come to think of it, I've encountered just about every flavor you can imagine. I've been in churches where the people shouted praise and in others where they whispered prayers. Some kneel at their pews, others stand with their hands lifted, while another group simply bows their heads. Some sing contemporary choruses and others prefer the old hymns. There really are a lot of flavors out there.

Which flavor is the best? It depends on who you ask. The Red Zingers think the Earl Grey crowd is too stuffy, while the Earl Grey crowd believes the Red Zingers are too wild. They both think the Country Apples aren't educated enough while they are convinced that the other groups put far too much confidence in the wisdom of man. This is sort of silly, isn't it? Yet those are the exact attitudes often present in the body of Christ.

God's family is a diverse family. There is a world full of people around us who need the life of Jesus. Like you and me, each person finds certain flavors distasteful and others to be more palatable. The different flavors represent the variety within the church. Contrary to the opinion of many Christians, *there is no best flavor.* The flavor is not the important element. What really matters is the water. If the pitcher (Christian) is filled with water (Jesus), the flavor (personality) of the tea doesn't really matter. Some people will be drawn to Christ because of the appeal of one flavor, while other unsaved people will be more receptive to another. As long as they receive the Water of Life, what difference does the flavor make? The Holy Spirit uses the distinctive flavors found in the body of Christ to reach the world. Regardless of our own particular flavor, every Christian can cry out to the world, "Oh taste and see that the LORD is good" (Psalm 34:8)!

• • •

Dear Father,
Thank You for giving me righteousness in Jesus Christ. Renew my mind so that I might begin to see myself as You see me. Transform my thoughts to conform with the truth of Your Word. I acknowledge that You have made me totally righteous in Christ. Cause me to walk in the truth of my identity even when I don't feel like a righteous person. Your life has permeated my being, Lord. By faith I believe it—make it real in my emotions in Your timing.

G.R.A.C.E. Group Questions

1. Read 1 Peter 4:12-13. What benefit is to be derived from problems in the life of a Christian? What does this passage mean when it talks about "the revelation of His glory"?

2. In 1 Corinthians 6:17, the Bible says that believers have been joined together with Christ and made one spirit with Him. What does this mean?

3. What does it mean to be filled with the Spirit? (Ephesians 5:18).

4. What would you say to a person who says, "I am trying to be righteous"? What verses from the Bible would you show him?

5. What is the difference between positional righteousness and literal righteousness? Which viewpoint do you believe?

6. Just as there are many flavors of tea, so there are churches with diverse types of personality and style. Which one is the best? Describe the flavor of the church that you prefer. List three positive aspects of a flavor that you don't particularly like.

4

Say Goodbye to Mr. Law

I WANT TO BE a better husband," Carl said to me while glancing over at his wife, Katie. "I know that I have an explosive temper and I really do try to control it," he continued. As he spoke, Katie sat by his side, slightly turned away from him. Pools of tears filled her eyes as she listened to him talk. Finally she spoke. "Steve, I don't doubt that he tries to control his temper. But the bottom line is, he isn't succeeding, and I'm getting tired of his sarcastic criticism."

The people before me were Christians. They were actively involved in their church, and they had a son about to go away to college to prepare for the ministry. Yet I have never met two people who were more defeated than they. In spite of all the outward indicators of successful Christian lives, their marriage had hit rock bottom.

Carl had never been physically abusive to his wife, but his verbal abuse had driven her to the place of despair. He had promised repeatedly to change the impatient, critical demeanor he had toward her. I believed that he sincerely wanted to overcome the sin of anger, but he just couldn't do it. With all of his good intentions, spiritual disciplines, and promises to God, he was still enslaved to a sin from which he could not experience freedom.

Methods for Overcoming Sins

As I listened to Carl explain his despair over his inability to control his temper and his tongue, I asked him how he had approached the problem until now. He told how he had read books written by Christians about over-coming anger. Some mornings he would awaken and promise himself that he wouldn't say anything critical regardless of how he felt about Katie's actions that day. "Those are usually our worst days," he said with obvious desperation. He had memorized Bible verses dealing with patience and love. In an effort to suppress his feelings, he would often quote the verses when he felt angry. But none of these methods seemed to work.

In the weeks to come, Carl would discover that his impasse with his own anger was a result of the methods he used to deal with it. The problem wasn't that he used the wrong methods. The cause for his continued defeat was that he believed victory over sin could come through *any* method. Contrary to what many Christians believe, victory over sin doesn't come by the right *method,* even one that we believe is from the Bible. Rather, victory is found in the Person of Jesus Christ. The apostle Paul said that God "gives us the victory through our Lord Jesus Christ" (1 Corinthians 15:57). No method will give real victory over sin.

Even if Carl had been able to suppress the expression of his anger, it would have found an outlet in some other way. Maybe he would have become depressed. Maybe he would have become bitter toward Katie. Or maybe he would have become proud of being such a good Christian that he could overcome anger. He simply would have traded one sin for another.

Trying to overcome sin by changing one's behavior is typical of a person whose life is ruled by law. Remember that law is a system whereby someone tries to make spiritual progress or gain God's blessings based on what he does. In a life where grace rules, victory over sin is experienced by the expression of the indwelling Christ within us. The mere absence of expressed sin is not victory. Jesus Christ within us is our victory. Until a Christian understands his union with Christ, his default setting will be a legalistic lifestyle. His whole life will revolve around rules.

Committing Spiritual Adultery

How would you define the meaning of spiritual adultery? Many Christians suggest that spiritual adultery occurs when a believer sins. While we wouldn't argue with that definition, it doesn't go far enough. Spiritual adultery can exist in the life of a person who is committing no known sins. Paul describes its meaning in Romans 7:1-4:

> Or do you not know, brethren (for I am speaking to those who know the law), that the law has jurisdiction over a person as long as he lives? For the married woman is bound by law to her husband while he is living; but if her husband dies, she is released from the law concerning the husband. So then if, while her husband is living, she is joined to another man, she shall be called an adulteress; but if her husband dies, she is free from the law, so that she is not an adulteress, though she is joined to

> another man. Therefore, my brethren, you also
> were made to die to the Law through the body
> of Christ, that you might be joined to another,
> to Him who was raised from the dead, that we
> might bear fruit for God.

Paul uses the model of marriage to teach about the relationship between the Christian and rules. He says that if a woman is married to a man, she is bound to him as long as he lives. If she leaves him for another man she becomes an adulteress, because the only way out of a marriage is by death.

Each of us was born into this world with a spiritual mate. We were born married to the system of Law. We became joined to this system in the garden of Eden when Adam ate from the tree of the knowledge of good and evil. Because we were in Adam, his marriage to Law became our own. Before we became Christians, Law was our husband. He gave us the rules of right and wrong, and his goal is to keep us following those rules.

Nag, Nag, Nag!

After a while, we grow weary with a mate who always critiques our every move. We find ourselves wanting to lash out at that mate, pointing out his faults. Yet there is a problem when one is married to Law: He has no faults. In fact, the psalmist said that "the law of the Lord is perfect" (Psalm 19:7). Although perfect, Mr. Law shows no compassion whatsoever. He tells us everything to do, but won't lift a finger to help us. He is quick to point it out when we fail. His whole demeanor in relating to us is one of condemnation and death (see 2 Corinthians 3:7-9). It is a miserable existence, but there is nothing we can do to get out of this relationship. Marriage is "until death do us part," and he is never going to die.

Meanwhile, in eternity, God looks down on you. He is thinking how much He would like for you to be His wife. "Oh, if I were married to you, I would treat you differently," He might say. "I would simply love you and wouldn't be demanding like Mr. Law has been." Yet the problem remains. We are born married to Law. So from the eternal vantage point, God devised a plan. In order to get you out of the marriage to Law, He planned and carried out a death. It wasn't Law that died, but instead, God worked it out so that *you* died. How did that happen? God placed you into Jesus Christ on the cross! There the person who was married to Law died. Then after your death, He allowed you to be born again. In this new life, you are married to Mr. Grace—Jesus! This is exactly what Paul meant in Romans 7:4 when he said that we died through the body of Christ so that we might be joined to Jesus!

---

*Jesus says,
"I want you to receive and
enjoy My love!" But we say,
"I understand that part, Lord.
But what do you want me to do?"*

Oh, how different things are being married to Jesus! He always acts in love toward us. He is thrilled that we are His. The groom wants just one thing from His bride— that she eagerly receive His love! Anything that He calls upon us to do, He ends up doing Himself! (see 1 Thessalonians 5:24). If He ever asks us to carry a burden, He sweeps us off our feet and carries us! Ephesians 1:7-8 says that He has lavished the riches of His grace upon us. He never condemns us (Romans 8:1), but always affirms and lovingly guides us. He anticipates the eternal honeymoon which He will enjoy with us.

Not all is perfect in this marriage made in heaven, however. Sometimes you may be confused about your role as the bride of Christ. It is true that at salvation, the old you who was married to Law died. Now you are a brand new person. Paul said you are "a new creature" and that "the old things passed away" (2 Corinthians 5:17). However, despite the fact that you have a brand new nature, you still have the same brain in your skull. If you don't understand the fact that you have no relationship to Law anymore, there will be an inclination to attempt to relate to Mr. Grace (Jesus) in the same way in which you related to Law.

A Christian who doesn't understand his identity in Christ might ask, "Jesus, what do You want me to do?" To which He could respond, "I want you to receive and enjoy My love!" "Yes," we might answer, "but what do You want me to *do*?" "I want you to receive My love," He could again say. "I understand that part, Lord. But what do you want me *to do*?"

Do you see where the problem arises? Until a person knows that he has died to the law, he will attempt to relate to Jesus through the law system. That will never work. God's primary concern is not our *doing*, but our *being*. He knows that when we understand who we are, then the doing of the Christian life will naturally flow from that revelation. Grace focuses on being, while law focuses on doing. Some have suggested that many of us should be called "human doings" instead of "human beings" because of our obsession with doing. When grace rules, the doing will fall into place. However, God's primary purpose in salvation is that we "may know . . . the only true God, and Jesus Christ whom [He] hast sent" (John 17:3). When we know Him intimately, we will *want* to do those things which glorify Him.

How Adultery Happens

When a Christian gets frustrated because Jesus won't give him a list of rules, he may turn back to Law and ask, "Will *you* tell me what to do?" Mr. Law is always ready to make a connection with a Christian with wandering eyes—one who looks away from Jesus. So a believer may find himself married to Mr. Grace (Jesus) and yet involved again with Mr. Law. What is it called when a person is married to one partner but involved with another? *Spiritual adultery.* That's what a Christian has when he builds his life around rules. The Bible clearly teaches that we are dead to the law. We have no relationship with rules anymore. Our life is Jesus Christ.

What Will Make Me Behave?

Some Christians find it scary to think that they are totally free from a system of rules. When I first began to understand grace for the Christian, I was afraid that I might become derelict in my responsibilities as a believer. I even thought that without rules, I might begin to minimize the seriousness of sin in my own life. I came to discover that I had found a security in my religious rules. When I kept them, I felt everything was all right with me spiritually. When I sensed any sort of spiritual deficit in my life, I would mentally run down the checklist of rules to see which one I was failing. But when a person examines himself to see if he is living up to the law, he will *always* discover areas of inconsistency. I thought the answer was to renew my efforts to do more. Yet even when I poured my energies into keeping these self-imposed laws, I wasn't really experiencing the life God intends.

The apostle Paul walked the same legalistic road as many of us. He mentioned how he had believed that he could experience life to the fullest if he only did the right things. Yet he said that when he embraced any commandment to find life, it "proved to result in death for me" (Romans 7:10). There is no list of rules one may follow and experience life. A Christian may believe his frustration comes because he doesn't adequately live up to certain rules, but the real problem is that he is focusing on rules at all.

> *We must recognize that the tree of knowledge of good and evil can be the source of good as well as evil.*

Galatians 3:21-22 says, "If a law had been given which was able to impart life, then righteousness would indeed have been based on the law. But the Scripture has shut up all men under sin, that the promise by faith in Jesus Christ might be given to those who believe." It is important to remember that living by law doesn't necessarily mean that you focus on the law found in Scripture. Like the Pharisees, many people have gone beyond the Bible and created their own laws. A lifestyle ruled by law is one where the focus is on performance. It is a lifestyle which is obsessed with doing the right thing instead of being obsessed with Jesus.

Stay Off the Law Tree

When God placed Adam and Eve in the garden of Eden, he specifically told them not to eat from the tree of the knowledge of good and evil. His plan was that they would ultimately live from the tree of life, which represents Jesus Christ—who *is* life. Yet man chose to disobey and eat from the forbidden tree. The tree of the knowledge of good and evil could be called "the law tree" because it offered knowledge about the rules of right and wrong. When Adam ate from that tree, he instantly found himself at a place where doing right and avoiding wrong became the defining issue of life. Until that point, his behavior had always glorified God because he had walked with the Lord daily, depending entirely on Him for every detail in life. Now his focus was on his behavior, not God.

Jesus came to rectify the damage caused by Adam's sin. Until the fall, the only thing that mattered was that Adam and Eve were living in total dependence upon God. After their sin, the primary matter became that of doing right. Through the cross, however, we can be restored to the place of intimacy which Adam forfeited. As a result, the criterion for our lives returns to God's original design: living in total dependence on Him at every moment. The New Testament calls it *abiding* in Christ. When a Christian focuses on doing right and avoiding wrong, he is completely missing the point of the cross as it relates to his lifestyle. He is functioning from the law tree, not life.

Doing Good Can Be a Sin

In order to better understand what it means for a person's life to be ruled by laws, consider this illustration: Pretend that one morning, after he had eaten from the law tree, Adam woke up because his wife, Eve, was leaning over him and kissing him gently on the cheek. "Good morning, my sweetheart," she whispered. "I brought you breakfast in bed this morning. You seemed to be resting so well that I let you sleep late today." Adam opened his eyes, took one look at Eve, and snarled at her in anger, "What do you mean waking me up, woman? Couldn't you see that I was asleep? How dare you! What have you shoved under my nose . . . a bowl of fruit? You've already caused me enough trouble with fruit! Get out of my face!" Shocked, Eve's eyes filled with tears and she ran off to a secluded place where she could cry alone.

By mid-morning Adam was feeling guilty about how he had treated his wife. He found her and humbly approached her. "Eve, I am so sorry. It was so wrong for me to behave that way. It was simply *evil*! Please forgive me. I wouldn't blame you if you left me for another . . . well, anyway, you get the point." Eve looked up through teary eyes as Adam continued. "Eve, I'm going to make it up to you, I promise. Tomorrow will be your special day. Listen, world! Tomorrow is Eve Day on planet earth," he shouted. True to his word, the next day Adam treated Eve like a queen. He pampered her all day long. That night when she went to bed, he gently leaned across her, kissed her on the cheek, and said, "Good night, my dear princess. I'm so blessed to have you as my wife."

"Oh Adam, you're so good to me," she cooed.

Now let's see how much we understand about legalism. There are only two questions on this test. Our answers to these questions will reveal whether we tend to see the Christian life primarily from a standpoint of law or grace. Ready?

1. Was God pleased with Adam on the first day in the story?

2. Was God pleased with Adam on the second day in the story?

The answer to both questions is no. God was not pleased on either day. Adam's behavior was evil on the first day and good on the second day. However, we must recognize that the tree of the knowledge of good and evil can be the source of good *as well as* evil. Although Adam's behavior changed from one day to the next, he still had the same problem. *On both days he was up the wrong tree!*

When law rules a Christian, his focus is on improving his behavior. Yet even if he does manage to improve his behavior, what has he accomplished spiritually? Even an unsaved person can often improve his performance. Jesus didn't give the gift of salvation merely to help us perform better. He came to earth so that we might have an abundant *life!* (see John 10:10). There are many miserable Christians who have exemplary behavior, but joy doesn't come by doing the right thing. In a lifestyle where grace rules, *Jesus* is the source of joy.

Even when a person does good, his actions may still be sin. Only those actions which are animated by the life of Jesus within us have real value. When we live in total dependence on Jesus within us, we are walking in faith and will always glorify God. When we focus on improving our behavior, we are not walking in faith. Hebrews 11:6 plainly says, "Without faith it is impossible to please Him." The Bible says that whatever is not of faith is sin. So a person may do something good and his action could still be a sin because it isn't done in faith. Someone has rightly said that God doesn't appreciate what He doesn't initiate.

Christians Don't Need the Law

Paul clearly asserted that we were made to die to the law so that we might be joined to Christ. What relationship does the Christian have, then, to a system of rules which govern behavior? Absolutely none! When you were saved, you were "made to die to the Law through the body of Christ, that you might be joined to another, to Him who was raised from the dead" (Romans 7:4). Having been given the resurrection life of Jesus Christ, you don't need the law anymore. You have Jesus Christ living within to guide your steps.

"Don't we need to commit ourselves to the laws of God?" a person might ask. That's like asking if we should commit ourselves to someone other than our own mate. We have died to the rules system. The law still exists, but it isn't intended for those of us who have received the righteous nature of Jesus Christ.

Paul said in 1 Timothy 1:8-10:

> We know that the Law is good, if one uses it lawfully, realizing the fact that *law is not made for a righteous man*, but for those who are lawless and rebellious, for the ungodly and sinners, for the unholy and profane, for those who kill their fathers or mothers, for murderers and immoral men and homosexuals and kidnappers and liars and perjurers, and whatever else is contrary to sound teaching . . . (emphasis added).

We have already learned in chapter four that Christians are righteous people who have the nature of Jesus Christ. To accept what Paul says about the law in this verse demands that we acknowledge that we have no relationship to rules. Our lifestyle isn't governed by rules, but relationship. We aren't motivated by laws, but love!

My wife, Melanie, and I have four children. In the places where we have lived while rearing them, there are laws governing the responsibilities of parents. These laws are a part of the penal code to ensure that children receive proper care. If parents break these laws, there is the risk that their children will be taken out of their home. In fact, if a violation of the law is severe enough, the parents might even go to jail.

I must confess that during all our years of child rearing, we have never been to the courthouse to read those laws on the books. There are probably hundreds of laws concerning parental responsibilities recorded there, but we've never read even one. One might wonder if we weren't afraid that we might break the law and have our children taken away from us. Yet that thought never crossed our minds once. Although I have never read those laws, I can confidently assert that we have fulfilled every one of them. In fact, we have gone above and beyond what the law requires. Do you know why? It's because we have related to our children on the basis of love! Love for Andrew, Amy, David, and Amber caused us to care for them in a way that far surpasses the minimum requirements of the law. Those laws are indeed on the books and they serve a useful purpose, but they have nothing to do with me. The only people that come to interact with those laws are the people who neglect or abuse their children. Melanie and I don't need them; we love our children.

When grace rules a person's life, he will find that his actions will be motivated by love for Jesus Christ. The driving force of his life won't be duty, but desire. He will crawl out from under the heavy weight of *ought to* and start living from a *want to* motivation. He won't have a reckless disregard for religious laws. He simply won't have *any* regard for religious laws.

Now, that kind of statement might startle some people. "Antinomianism!" some theologian might cry. (For the rest of us, the word simply describes one who is against law.) I don't advocate being against the laws of God, but merely want to point out that the law was not given for those of us who are saved. In the next chapter, we will consider the purpose of the law. Suffice it to say at this point that the law is not given for righteous people—which includes you if you have received Jesus Christ.

Why Do We Still Live by Rules?

The Bible clearly teaches that we died to the law. Why, then, do so many Christians today still try to build a lifestyle around rules? Paul deals with this question and bluntly answers it in Colossians 2:20-23:

> If you have died with Christ to the elementary principles of the world, why, as if you were living in the world, do you submit yourself to decrees, such as, "Do not handle, do not taste, do not touch!" (which all refer to things destined to perish with the using)—in accordance with the commandments and teachings of men? These are matters which have, to be sure, the appearance of wisdom in self-made religion and self-abasement and severe treatment

of the body, but are of no value against fleshly indulgence.

Here Paul asks a pointed question that presses hard against those embracing legalism. He begins by again emphasizing that believers have *died* to the religious rules system that governs the rest of the world. This is the same point he made in Romans 7:5 when he stated that we were made to die to the law in the body of Christ so that we might be released from law and joined to Him.

Those who believe that a person who emphasizes God's grace over God's laws will run wild, have a common misunderstanding about salvation. True Christians don't want to run wild.

The next question is an obvious one which demands an answer from many in the contemporary church: Why are you acting like you are still a part of the world by submitting yourself to all these regulations? How would you answer that question? Do you understand that when you were saved, God set you free from the rules system so that you could experience Christ as your life? If so, why do you think you still need rules?

As I explained this biblical truth to a fellow named Hank, he argued, "But Steve, you don't understand! God gave us His law and we must obey it! Without God's laws, people would run wild!" Hank's concern reflected a common misunderstanding about salvation. He failed to recognize that Christians don't *want* to run wild. The presence of Jesus within us changes our desires! John said it like this: "No one who is born of God [habitually] practices sin, because His seed abides in him; and he cannot [habitually practice] sin, because he is born of God" (1 John 3:9). God's seed is Jesus. He lives inside the Christian; consequently, it is totally out of character for the saint to sin. Believers who think they can live a lifestyle of habitual sin will ultimately find themselves suffocating in its stinking stench. It is exciting to run into the sin house, but a Christian will soon find himself inwardly screaming, "I've got to get out of here!"

So why do many Christians live by laws? In Colossians 2:23, Paul says it is because "these are matters which have, to be sure, the appearance of wisdom in self-made religion. . . ." The religionist loves rules for one simple reason—they make him look good. It's all about appearance. A legalist enjoys the special status he holds among his peers because he seems to keep all the right rules. It is a matter of pride.

It is interesting to discover that among the various camps of legalism, different sets of rules are held in high esteem. One group is known by the things they do, while another group is known by the things they don't do. Yet in each clan, those held in highest regard are the ones who are the best at keeping the particular esoteric rules of their group. The sad irony of their diligent focus on behavior is that their rules "are of no value against fleshly indulgence" (Colossians 3:23). In other words, a ton of rules don't provide an ounce of prevention against sin. To the contrary, rules actually impede our spiritual walk in a way that most Christians would never imagine.

• • •

Dear Father,

I realize that I have misunderstood how You have designed for me to live my life. I have been focusing on rules. Unintentionally, I have committed spiritual adultery. Now I see the truth that You have set me free from the law so that I might experience and fully enjoy Your life. I affirm that I am dead to the law and am now married to Jesus. Teach me to allow my lifestyle to flow from my relationship to You. I love You, Jesus. Renew my mind in this area so that I might walk in the complete freedom You have already given me through the cross.

G.R.A.C.E. Group Questions

1. At the beginning of the chapter, Steve described Carl's predicament over his anger. None of the methods he tried seemed to work. Discuss some of the common methods that Christians use to try to overcome sins. Having read this chapter, what would you tell Carl about his problem with anger?

2. Read Romans 7:1-5. What is spiritual adultery? What relationship does the believer have to rules? Describe ways that you have committed spiritual adultery. How did we get out of our marriage to Mr. Law?

3. Describe the process that leads to a Christian committing spiritual adultery.

4. How can it be a sin when a Christian does a good thing? Describe the differences between the law tree and the life tree.

5. Do Christians need the law? Why or why not? Discuss the meaning of 1 Timothy 1:8-10. For whom is the law given? If we as believers don't focus on religious laws, what will govern our behavior?

6. Read Colossians 2:20-23. Why do Christians try to build their lifestyle around a set of rules? List some rules that you have embraced in your own life.

5

Sin's
Secret Weapon

*L*ORD, I DON'T understand myself. I honestly want to be a godly husband and dad. What's wrong with me? I can't even do the most basic things necessary to be a good Christian!" The year was 1988. These were the words I wrote in my spiritual journal on January 16. I remember well my frustration. Actually, it was more than frustration. At the time, I loathed myself because of the inconsistency I saw in my life.

A few weeks earlier I had done what I had always done at the beginning of a new year. I wrote my new year's resolutions. My commitments at the beginning of every new year always included promises to myself about spiritual disciplines for the coming year. One of my promises to myself for 1988 was that I would read the Bible and pray with my family *every single day* of the year, without fail. I had reasoned that, unlike previous years, this time I *really* meant it. I would do it this time. I *must* do it this time!

Yet here I was less than three weeks later, having neglected for the past two days the very thing I had *promised* that I would not miss for 365 days. Failing to have devotional time with my family every day was just one of the areas where I struggled with consistency. It seemed that every time I identified an area where I wanted to improve my Christian life, things seemed to get worse instead of better. My failure seemed to always be in direct proportion to my efforts to succeed.

Sin's Secret Power

There is a little-known reason why Christians find themselves in the place of failure after having tried with such sincerity to live a successful Christian life. It is almost as if Satan has a secret weapon that many believers don't know about. A Christian may start moving forward with perfectly pure intentions and with a proper motivation, then suddenly find himself lying flat on his back on the spiritual battlefield. When I resolved to pray and read the Bible with my family every day, I was totally sincere. Yet within three weeks, I was shot down. Can you relate to the experience of earnestly setting out to do that which would glorify God only to soon find yourself defeated? You may be a victim of sin's secret power. What is this weapon that few Christians recognize?

It is the attempt to embrace religious rules. The Bible calls these rules *the law*. Law is the Trojan horse which has infiltrated the contemporary church with devastating results. Religious rules *look* so compatible with the Christian life that many never suspect their deadly effect until they become victims. Most Christians fail to see the enemy approaching because he is dressed up in such an attractive suit of clothes, which constitute the law. Yet beneath the moral veneer of his appearance lies a sinister force which catches the unsuspecting saint off guard.

Now, don't get the idea that I am demeaning the place of law. There is nothing wrong with it in its proper place. Its place just isn't for those of us who are saved. When the law connects with those for whom it is intended, it does its job in a superb way. The trouble is that it will have the same effect on Christians when we connect with it.

What does the law do in the life of a person? It surprises many Christians to discover that rules don't curb sin, they stir it up. Romans 5:20 says "The Law came in that the transgression might increase." Do you believe that God gave the law so that people would keep it? That is not its purpose. The Bible clearly teaches that the purpose of the law is to reveal sin. It doesn't *generate* sin, but it does most definitely *stimulate* it within any person who embraces it. It brings it from beneath the surface right out into the open. First Corinthians 15:56 says that "the power of sin is the law." Rules don't keep a person from sinning; they *cause* him to sin!

---

*Religious rules look so compatible with
the Christian life that many
never suspect their deadly effect
until they become victims.*

So the unwitting Christian who determines to build his life around spiritual rules is setting himself up for a lifestyle filled with failure! There certainly is nothing wrong with a man praying and reading the Bible with his family, but when I wrote my own ten commandments at the beginning of each new year, I immediately set myself up for failure. Law didn't care how sincere I was when I wrote, "Thou shalt have family altar every day this year." It still did its job, and 16 days later it was all over except the crying.

Stepping Back Through Time

Consider the origin of the codified law of God. While the law system started in the garden at the tree of the knowledge of good and evil, the written laws were not given until Mount Sinai. Why did God give His written law to mankind? Being omniscient, it isn't possible that He thought man would keep it. So if He knew that man wasn't going to keep His laws before He even gave them, why did he do it?

Allow me to take literary liberty at this point by asking you to use your imagination. Let's step back into a time in history when man is whining to God about his inability to please God by his behavior. The conversation might have gone like this:

"Lord, it seems we can't please You regardless of what we do. What do You want from us?" "I want you to trust Me and allow Me to guide you moment by moment," God answered. "God, we have the cause of this problem figured out. If You will just tell us what to *do*, then we can do it and everything will be okay." "No," answered God, "it isn't a matter of your doing. The issue is one of *trusting*. Just trust Me." "No, Lord. Just give us a list of rules. What would it take to be right with You?" "I don't want to give you a list. I want you to trust Me," God answered. "Lord, give us the list!" Israel demanded. "I would really prefer that you just trust Me," God answered again. "Give us the list. Tell us what to do! Just tell us what to do!" they insisted.

Finally there came a point in time when God gave the written law. "I've jotted down a few things here that reflect My eternal purity." "Give them to us! We will do them. Finally, we will know what to *do*. Give us the list. Give it here." So on Mount Sinai God handed Israel the law through the prophet Moses. Looking at the demands of the law, Israel immediately responded, "We can't do that!" "Exactly," God said.

God didn't think for one moment that man would keep the law. Remember, He knows everything. He didn't give the law because *He* believed man would keep it, but rather because *man* believed he could keep it. He mistakenly believed that if he had clear instructions, he could achieve a righteous standing with God on the basis of his behavior. So God gave the law to demonstrate that righteousness can never come by adherence to religious rules. The law is intended to frustrate us to the point of despair so that we give up all hope that we can successfully live in a way that pleases God. By forcing us to admit our own inability to accomplish a righteous lifestyle, it drives us toward Jesus so that we can *accept* righteousness from Him as a gift. The purpose of the law is to inflame sin, thus causing us to see our own hopelessness apart from the mercy and grace of God expressed to us through Jesus Christ.

Legalistic Discipleship

Every Christian understands that it is impossible to be saved by keeping religious rules. Yet many think that once a person becomes a Christian, the strategy changes. Let's walk through the commonly used approach in leading Bill to faith in Christ and then starting to "disciple" him after his conversion.

"Bill, you simply need to trust Jesus to save you. That's all that is necessary. What? Stop your bad habits? No, Bill. You don't understand. You don't need to do anything to be saved. Just trust Jesus. What? Start attending church? No, my friend! Just place your faith in Christ and receive

Him. Clean up your language? Bill, you're missing the point. This isn't about what *you* do; it is about what *He* has done. Becoming a Christian is *all* Him! Just trust Him. Just believe. It's by faith, Bill. It's not through doing anything. It's Him alone!"

> *Teach a man who he is in Christ and he can't be stopped from godly activity. Try to control him through rules, and you set him up for spiritual ruin.*

Then Bill trusts Christ and is born again . . .

"God bless you, Bill! I am so glad that you have trusted Christ. Now that you're a Christian, I know you want to get started right, don't you? Let me tell you a few things that will help you get started in your Christian life. First, you must to come to church Sunday morning and let the pastor know you have been saved. Then you have to be baptized and join the church. You should attend all the services, including Sunday night and Wednesday night. You also ought to become a part of the men's mission group. And our outreach visitation on Tuesdays too. Can you sing? If so, you really ought to join the choir. Oh, don't forget our home study group. And here's an absolute *must*, Bill—you need to get into the Bible. Read three chapters in the Old Testament and two in the New and you'll go through your whole Bible every year that way. And don't forget about prayer—you should pray about 30 minutes every morning. Oh yes, did I mention tithing? . . . "Is it any wonder that the Bills we reach ultimately go running out the back door of the church when nobody is watching? We *say* that we recognize the Christian life is a walk in grace, but our approach to discipleship often reveals a not-so-subtle legalism that ultimately sucks the vitality out of new Christians. Having served as a pastor for over 20 years, I've seen many press the eject button and disappear from church a short time after receiving Christ. Others who remained ended up looking like they had a legalism lobotomy. They still went through the motions of Christian living, but without any sense of life in their activity.

When grace rules a believer's life, he won't need a religious Gestapo to police his actions or dictate his behavior. Discipleship is important, but biblical discipleship means strengthening a person in an understanding of what it means to be in Christ, not indoctrinating him with religious rules. Teach a man who he is in Christ, and he can't be stopped from godly activity. Try to control him through rules, and you set him up for spiritual ruin. We weren't called to a spiritual list, but rather to a spiritual rest. Jesus said that those who come to him will receive rest (see Matthew 11:28). That kind of statement scares the legalist; he immediately becomes afraid that if a person embraces a position of rest, he may become passive.

Does Grace Produce Passivity?

"If I teach people that the Christian life is one of rest, won't some people misapply the truth and become lazy?" Ted asked me. I understood his concern. Ted, a pastor, feared that his congregation might become lethargic if he began to teach the grace walk to them. "Ted," I answered, "any time we teach biblical truth, there is the risk that some people will distort what we have taught and misapply it to their lives. However, that doesn't mean that we should avoid biblical truths simply because someone might pervert what the Bible says." Ted's fear is understandable; I had the same concerns when I was a pastor. I was afraid that if I taught people that they were free from obligation and were simply called to enjoy Jesus and abide in Him at every moment, they might not do the things that needed to be done to keep the church functioning. I was afraid that teaching grace might produce passivity.

In reality, resting in Christ never leads a person to laziness. Abiding in Jesus means to completely depend on Him to animate our lifestyle—to continually trust Him to express His life through us. When a person chooses to live in that mode, there is absolutely no way that he will become passive! Grace is not a license to be lazy. To the contrary, it is the divine enablement to courageously and powerfully live out who we are! That doesn't mean that we will fulfill all the expectations of the religious legalist who seeks to impose his own "To-Do List" upon us, but it does mean that our lifestyle will express the activity of Jesus through us.

A Christian who is energized by the life of Jesus Christ is an active person. Yet his activity isn't generated by self effort, but by Jesus Himself. Some modern methods of discipleship imply that while we are saved by grace, it is up to us to grow by our own efforts. Yet we are to walk the Christian life in the same way that we entered in—by faith. "We walk by faith" is Paul's summary of our new life (2 Corinthians 5:7).

Grace Creates Godly Desires

Legalistic discipleship emphasizes *obligation* in the Christian life. Grace focuses on *opportunities* to express the Christ life. A life ruled by law is driven by duty. A lifestyle where grace rules is led by desire.

Remember Bill, whom we brought to Christ, then suffocated with rules after he was saved? Our approach to him is a description of the typical approach in many churches. Before a person is saved, we tell him, "It's all Jesus. It's all Him. This isn't about you. It's *all* Him!" Then as soon as he trusts Christ, we begin to teach, "Now it's up to *you*. It's about what *you* do for Him." Before salvation we affirm "It's faith. Faith! Faith!" Then the moment someone is born again, we stress, "It is works. Works! Works!" What a contradiction! Paul said, "As you therefore have received Christ Jesus the Lord, *so walk in Him*" (Colossians 2:6, emphasis added). The Bible teaches that we are to walk as Christians in the same way we entered in from the beginning—through appropriating His grace by faith!

A legalistic methodology in discipleship stems from the foundation of fear. It is the fear that Christians won't actually live a godly life apart from the coercive or persuasive pressure normally associated with rules. Yet genuine grace will motivate a man to live a godly lifestyle more than a thousand laws could ever do. A legalist greatly underestimates the power of the indwelling Holy Spirit. When a Christian knows that he is free from the law, he will discover that God's indwelling Spirit will motivate him to serve based on his relationship to Jesus, not because of external demands to perform.

Even in the ancient days of Ezekiel, God held forth the promise of the day of grace in which we live. Speaking through the prophet, he said:

> Moreover, I will give you a new heart and
> put a new spirit within you; and I will remove

> the heart of stone from your flesh and give you
> a heart of flesh. And I will put My Spirit within
> you and cause you to walk in My statutes, and
> you will be careful to observe My ordinances
> (Ezekiel 36:26-27).

Millenniums ago God knew what He was going to one day do through grace. Ezekiel predicted a day when those who knew God would be given a new heart and a new spirit. He anticipated the time when believers would experience an intrinsic motivation to serve God. No longer would those who knew Him respond to His commands from a sense of duty. A believer would have a new heart and would be motivated by desire. He would no longer *struggle* to live a godly lifestyle, keeping the commandments. Instead, the Spirit of God would come into man and *cause* God's people to carefully observe His commandments by simply resting in His empowering presence. Ezekiel predicted that in this new day those who followed God would no longer act on the basis of *external laws*, but rather would act out of the *internal life* they possessed.

We are now living in that day! A Christian whose life is ruled by grace is a motivated person. He actively serves and obeys God because he can't help but do so! Go ahead and try to stop him. It can't be done. He is a man on a mission and his mission is empowered by the omnipotent God of the universe who has taken up residence within him. Don't try telling a person walking in grace what he *must* do. He will tell you to keep your rules because he doesn't need them. He is motivated by a much higher and nobler source. The source of his behavior isn't some religious prescription; it is a real Person living within him, energizing and empowering him with divine life at every moment!

Rules Steal Our Victory

My family devotional rule stole my victory in that area of my life. Of course there is nothing wrong with a man leading his family in a devotional time together. However, when I placed myself under the *law* which insisted on strict observance to the family altar rule, that very law incited me to disobedience. That is the nature of religious rules. They always stir us to do the exact opposite of what they demand.

Have you ever been on a diet? If so, you should readily understand how law provokes a person to sin. A few years ago when I was approaching the age of 40, I couldn't stand the thought that my belt size and my age were approaching the same number! So I decided to do something about it. I enlisted in the battle of the bulge. (I didn't like the idea of being a Christian who *looks* like Buddha!) I initiated a "get tough policy" against my middle-age spread.

I normally eat pizza every now and then, but when I began this particular diet I determined that I would cut all pizza from my menu. Do you know how many fat grams and calories are in a pizza? It's obscene. So I decided, *No more pizza for me.* None. Not one slice. However, there was a slight barrier to overcome in order to successfully follow through with this decision. Three of my four children worked in a pizza restaurant. I'm talking brick-oven pizza. *Delicious* pizza. One of my sons cooked the pizza at this restaurant, so he was able to make our orders really special. He would load the pizza with cheese, smother it in pepperoni, and bake it with a thick crust. (I'm lusting even now as I think about it!)

I will not *eat pizza,* I told myself. Normally I would eat pizza maybe twice a month . . . until the diet began.

Suddenly I found myself consumed with the desire for brick-oven cooked pizza. I wanted it every day. In fact, every time I thought about my next meal, my mind screamed, *Pizza!* Pretty soon, it didn't take much for my mind to think of pizza when I saw anything that even remotely resembled pizza. One day I was driving through farmland in Iowa and thought I smelled pizza—then later I realized it was only a pig farm I was passing.

> Legalism presents the commandments
> as divine ultimatums coming from a
> harsh judge. "If you love Me, you had
> better keep My commandments."

The "thou shalt not eat pizza" law stirred within me a consuming hunger to eat it! That's what law does to our spiritual lives, too. Whether a person is a Christian or not, the law acts the same way upon everyone. It stirs up a person's passions to disobey. Paul described this perfectly in Romans 7:5 when he wrote, "While we were in the flesh, the sinful passions, which were *aroused* by the Law, were at work in the members of our body to bear fruit for death" (emphasis added). The passion to rebel is aroused by the law.

In the book *Pilgrim's Progress,* there is an incident where Christian goes into a great room that represents the human heart. The room is filled with dust, which represents sin. He takes a large broom (law) into the room and attempts to sweep out all the dust. But instead of sweeping away the dust, he simply stirs it up. That is the exact effect that law will have any time we attempt to use it as a means for eradicating sin.

What About the Commandments?

Since rules stimulate us to sin, what is the believer to do with the commandments of the New Testament? Didn't Jesus say that if we love Him, we will keep His commandments? (see John 14:15). He did indeed. Yet when grace rules a person's life, he will approach the commandments of the New Testament with a totally different attitude than the legalist. Legalism presents the commandments as divine ultimatums coming from a harsh Judge. When law rules a person, the tone of Jesus' words are heard like this: "If you love Me, you had better keep My commandments." By contrast, the grace walk causes the Christian to face the commandments with eager anticipation, not fear and intimidation. This believer understands the words of Jesus when He said, "If you love me, you will keep my commandments." When we love Jesus, we *will* keep His commandments. Obedience is the natural response of the Christian who loves Jesus. We have already learned that without love, the only thing we have to offer is lifeless compliance. Love is the basis for our obedience, not laws.

John stressed the relationship between love and our obedience to God's commandments when he said, "This is the love of God, that we keep His commandments; and His commandments are not burdensome" (1 John 5:3). It's not a strain for a Christian who is walking in grace to obey the commandments of God. It is a pleasure to be obedient!

As I write this chapter, I am in Pittsburgh, Pennsylvania, where I will spend the whole week. Suppose I were to ask for your advice concerning my responsibilities to my wife when I return home. How would you respond if I asked you whether or not I *must* kiss my wife when she picks me up at the airport on Saturday? What would you think if I were to seriously ask you what I *should* do when she greets me at the airport? You would probably assume that, because I asked a question like that, something must be wrong with my relationship with my wife. In a healthy marriage, a man wouldn't ask such a foolish question. The fact is that when I see Melanie on Saturday, I will kiss her. I can assure you that it won't be duty that motivates me. My love for my wife will animate my actions at that moment.

Thus the commandments of the New Testament do have a place in a life of grace. They present a beautiful blueprint that illustrates what a lifestyle looks like when it is empowered with the divine expression of the life of Jesus. When grace rules, we approach the Bible saying, "Lord, show me in Your Word all the ways that Jesus can express His life through me." Then when we come across commandments, we may exclaim with excitement, "Great! Here's a way that Christ can express His life through my lifestyle!" So the commandments are not a burden, but instead are a great blessing.

A New Motivation

Grace causes our motivation toward obedience to be love and desire. There was a time before we were saved when we had no inner desire to live a godly lifestyle. "But now we have been released from the Law, having died to that by which we were bound, so that we serve in newness of the Spirit and not in oldness of the letter" (Romans 7:6). In this newness of the Spirit, we remind ourselves that we died to the law and are no longer obligated to religious rules. Finally we are free to serve God because we *want* to, not because we have to.

Legalists, by contrast, aren't free to serve the Lord, they obligate themselves to.

"Ought to" is the ammunition for the legalist's gun. It will kill your joy every time it hits you. Is your life built around rules? Are you fulfilled in life? Sin's secret weapon is the power of the law, but our weapon against legalism is our love for Jesus Christ. While laws ultimately lead to certain failure, grace always produces the victory that only Christ can give.

• • •

Dear Father,

I acknowledge that I have often fallen victim to sin's secret weapon. The rules I have embraced have seemed so right to me. Yet now I realize that I will never experience Your life through rules. While I know that I was saved only because of Your grace, I have made the mistake of trying to move forward spiritually by my own works. I have trusted in my own self-discipline and not in the sufficiency of Your Life within me. Right now I affirm that You are my victory. Teach me to trust You and to be motivated by desire, not duty. I love You, Lord Jesus. May that be my motivation in life.

G.R.A.C.E. Group Questions

1. What is sin's secret power? Read Romans 7:5 and describe how laws affect the Christian. Discuss an example from your own life which illustrates how you set yourself up for failure by embracing a religious rule.

2. Why did God give the law even when He knew man would not keep it? Were people in the Old Testament saved by keeping the law? What purpose does the law serve today in the life of a believer? Of an unbeliever? What Bible verses substantiate your answers?

3. How would you describe legalistic discipleship? What are the elements of discipleship that are grounded in grace? Describe the discipleship program in your church.

4. What would you say to the person who expresses fear that teaching grace may encourage passivity? How would you answer the person who says, "I don't have to pray, read my Bible, or do anything else since I'm under grace."? What will keep a Christian from becoming passive when he understands grace?

5. Read Ezekiel 36:26-27. What does this verse mean when it speaks about us receiving a new spirit? How does God cause us to walk in His statutes? Do we play any part in this process? If so, what is our responsibility?

6. How do rules steal the Christian's victory? What rules can you identify which have robbed your victory? Were you taught certain rules as soon as you were saved? What are they?

7. What place do New Testament commandments have in the lives of Christians today? How do you interpret John 14:15? Discuss the difference between a legalistic understanding of this verse and an understanding based on grace.

6
Overcoming Our Sins

W HEN I WAS A YOUNG BOY, I loved to play marbles. I would often go out into the backyard and draw a circle in the dirt, put a handful of marbles "in the pot," and shoot marbles for hours. I often played with my friends, with each of us putting ten marbles in the circle and taking turns shooting. Did I play for keeps? Well, I'll just say that I had a *big* bag of marbles! I couldn't imagine a day ever coming when I gave up that hobby. I knew that one day I would grow old enough that I would look pretty silly on the ground with my favorite shooter, but I tried not to think about those days. I wanted to play forever.

One day while I was outside practicing, I heard someone call my name. I looked over toward the backyard of my friend, Phillip, and saw him there with Ricky and Danny. They were standing under a basketball hoop which hadn't been there the day before. "We're gonna play a game. We need a fourth man. Want to play?" they asked. I left my marbles in the dirt that day and never looked back. I had found a new passion. I loved to play basketball.

Every single day I couldn't wait to get home from school so that I could rush out into the backyard to play ball. Every day we would play until dark. Fridays were especially exciting—because we didn't have school the next day, our parents would often allow us to stay outside very late, shooting baskets when we could hardly even see the hoop. It was an adolescent boy's paradise.

Now this is something I can do all my life! I reasoned. *Mr. Lambert across the street still plays basketball and he's a grown man!* In those days I was convinced that there would never be a Friday night of my life when I didn't shoot basketball. I was addicted to it.

We don't experience victory by struggling against sins, but by setting our mind on Jesus.

One Sunday when I was barely 16 years old our family went to church. While sitting in the Sunday school class that morning, I noticed a new girl who walked into the class. I had never seen her before. I had never been on a date up to that time. When this girl walked past me, I checked her out—I mean, I *discerned* that this might be a good time to begin my dating life. I went home and asked my dad the big question. "Dad, if I get a date some Friday night, will you let me use your car to go out?" "Do you have a date?" my dad asked, probably glad to see his only son moving toward manhood. "Not yet," I answered. "But there's a girl I want to go out with if you'll let me use the car." "Who is she?" he asked. "A girl I met at church last week," I said. "Okay," he replied. "You can use the car if you get a date."

I couldn't wait until the next Sunday. As soon as church was over I made a beeline for this new girl. After some nervous small talk, I took the plunge. "Are you doing anything this Friday night?" I asked. "No," she answered, "why?" "Well, there's a new Barbra Streisand movie coming out this weekend. I thought we could go see it and then go over to Pizza Villa after the movie, if you want to," I said. "Sure, that sounds like fun," she said.

The following Friday night I picked her up and went out on my first date. It went very well. The next day my buddies all rushed over to my house bright and early. "Where were you?" they demanded to know. "We waited for you to come out. We play basketball *every* Friday!" they exclaimed with obvious irritation over my reckless disregard for our sacred routine. "Why didn't you join us?" Holding my shoulders back with my head held high, I answered, "Guys, I had a date!"

To their dismay, I called the girl and asked her to go out with me the following Friday. She accepted. In fact, I went out with her every Friday for the next three years, then I married her. We've been married since 1973. Now that I think about it, I can't remember the last time I played basketball on a Friday night. I had found something better!

Victory Over Sin Won't Come Through Discipline

When a person finds himself entangled with a sin, it is often difficult to imagine a time when he won't be connected to that sin. How does a person find freedom over habitual sins in his life? Certainly it won't happen by applying religious rules to his life. We have already seen how laws can actually arouse a person's desire to sin. The idea that a Christian should protect himself from sin by a strict adherence to rules is sin's secret weapon against the believer. Laws *always* stimulate sin.

I hate to compare wholesome activities like marbles and basketball to sin, but I want to use my experience with these as an analogy. If someone had told me when I was a young child that I would *have* to give up marbles, I would have resisted the idea. If someone had suggested that at age 16 I would be required to give up Friday night basketball, I would have rebelled against the very thought. As it was, I didn't focus on giving up either. I simply became obsessed with something else that I wanted more than those things. One might say that Melanie delivered me from basketball. It wasn't a struggle for me; I just set my mind on her and basketball sort of faded away.

That's how Jesus can deliver us from our sins! When we come to know who Jesus is in us and who we are in Him, we discover that sins we once couldn't imagine living without lose their appeal to us. We don't experience victory by struggling against sins, but by setting our mind on Jesus. The apostle Paul said it succinctly in Colossians 3:1-3:

> If then you have been raised up with Christ, keep seeking the things above, where Christ is, seated at the right hand of God. Set your mind on the things above, not on the things that are on earth. For you have died and your life is hidden with Christ in God.

We will never overcome sin through sheer determination and self-discipline. That kind of negative motivation keeps our eyes off Jesus and on our sins. We are to focus on Him, not sin! As we fall more and more in love with Jesus, those sins which we have so tightly caressed will become increasingly unattractive to us until we *want* to let them go.

When I was a child, we sometimes sang an old song that clearly teaches God's method for overcoming sin. It says, "Turn your eyes upon Jesus; look full in His wonderful face; and the things of earth will grow strangely dim in the light of His glory and grace." The repellent for sin is not self-effort. The remedy will always be nothing other than Jesus.

Reaping What We Sow

To think that concentrating on overcoming our sins will give us victory is a totally wrong approach to the matter. Not only will setting our mind on the flesh fail to bring victory, it will actually perpetuate our defeat. A legalist will always focus on behavior, but when grace rules we will focus on Jesus!

> Those who are according to the flesh set their minds on the things of the flesh, but those who are according to the Spirit, the things of the Spirit. For the mind set on the flesh is death, but the mind set on the Spirit is life and peace (Romans 8:5-6).

Paul asserts that whatever you set your mind upon will ultimately determine your behavior. If a man continually sets his mind on bass fishing, it will only be a matter of time before he is trying to figure out how to buy a bass boat. Those who set their minds on football usually can be found in front of the television on holidays, watching football—or, playing the game on a field with some friends.

If a person sets his mind on the sins of the flesh, he should not be surprised when his behavior matches his mindset. A person guarantees his own failure when he decides to overcome sin by concentrating on it. It will make no difference that he asks God to help him. God won't bless our efforts to deliver ourselves from sin after our salvation any more than He would help us overcome sin before we were saved. He wants us to realize that our attempts to achieve victory over sin are futile so that we will focus our attention toward Jesus. As long as we try to gain victory through our behavior, He will patiently wait until we have exhausted all our options. Then He will do for us what we can't do for ourselves. It is at that point that we are ready to receive His answer.

Lies That Bind

The first step in knowing how to experience freedom over sin is to understand the attitude of a Christian toward sin. Many believers who find themselves enslaved to a particular sin are under the mistaken belief that they love that sin. They assume that there is no way to be free from something that they love.

"I hate myself!" Those were the first words Jim spoke after our initial introduction to each other. He had scheduled an appointment with me to discuss "a personal problem." "Why do you hate yourself?" I asked him. As Jim began to explain his problem to me, I learned that he was addicted to pornography. "I can't help myself," he said. "I have come to love pornographic movies. I tell myself that I won't watch them anymore, but like clockwork I find myself back at the video store renting the under-the-counter videos that are available."

Jim was a victim of the same lie that keeps many Christians in bondage to sin. He confessed that he hated himself and loved the sin. In reality, Jim didn't even know himself. And he certainly didn't love the sin that had brought him to see me after coming to the place of absolute desperation. In the weeks ahead, I was able to share with Jim some truths that helped to set him free.

Jesus said, "You shall know the truth, and the truth shall make you free" (John 8:32). God's truth always sets people free. The implication of this statement is that if truth sets a person free, then lies bind a person. So to the extent that any Christian experiences bondage, he is believing a lie. But when he knows the truth, he discovers freedom.

Sin Is Repulsive to the Christian

Jim believed that he loved his secret sin. In reality, he didn't love it at all. He hated it. He had made the mistake of thinking that he loved his sin just because he kept indulging in it. If he had genuinely loved the sin, he never would have come to my office seeking help. He would have been perfectly content to continue in his sin. The reason for his emotional misery was because he was enslaved to a sin he hated.

The apostle Paul described his own encounter with sin, saying:

> For that which I am doing, I do not understand; for I am not practicing what I would like to do, but I am doing the very thing I hate... For the good that I wish, I do not do; but I practice the very evil that I do not wish (Romans 7:15,19).

Paul honestly confessed that he sinned. I'm glad he was honest about that. Don't ever think that you are the only one who has struggled with personal sins. The man who wrote most of the books in the New Testament openly admitted that he had seen days of great struggles with sin.

Paul affirmed that although he did sin, nothing in him loved it. The description of his attitude toward his own sins is given in Romans 7:15-25. After describing his struggle, he declares in verse 24: "Wretched man that I am! Who will set me free from the body of this death?" Paul experienced emotional distress because of sin. That will eventually be the experience of every Christian who struggles with sin.

Some people don't understand that it is possible to enjoy sin and hate it at the same time. If you didn't hate your sin, you wouldn't find yourself struggling with it.

Is there sin in your own life that comes to mind as you read these words? It is important for you to see your real attitude toward sin in order to be set free from its power. Don't be deceived into believing that you love sin just because you find yourself going back to it and finding it pleasurable. The Bible teaches that sin brings pleasure for a while but eventually it turns sour in the life of a believer. Some people don't understand that it is possible to enjoy sin and hate it at the same time. If you didn't hate your sin, you wouldn't find yourself struggling with it. The fact that you may enjoy it says nothing about you, but simply demonstrates that sin is pleasurable. Jim failed to understand this fact and had embraced the lie that he loved pornography.

Sin Is Resident in the Christian

Jim's declaration "I hate myself" reveals another lie he believed—a lie that kept him enslaved. He identified himself by the sin that held him. He believed that pornography was a part of who he was as a man. He made no distinction whatsoever between his sin and his identity as a man. Consequently, he saw himself as his own worst enemy.

Jim's misunderstanding is common among those who fail to understand their identity in Christ. Until a person knows who he is, his perception of himself will cause his behavior and identity to merge into one entity. Yet the Bible clearly teaches that when a Christian sins, his sin doesn't reflect who he is, but only how he behaves when he is not trusting Christ within him to animate his lifestyle.

In describing his own sinful behavior, Paul made two points clear. First, he expressed how much he hated his sin. Then he made a definite distinction between his own identity and the power of sin within him. Twice he asserted that when he sinned, it was no longer he who sinned, "but sin which dwells in me" (Romans 7:17, 20).

When Paul said that, was he trying to shirk responsibility for his sin? Was he suggesting, as some people do, that "the devil made me do it"? Absolutely not. Paul accepted full responsibility for the choices that he made. He was simply clarifying that when a Christian sins, it is a contradiction of his own nature. In his statements about sin, he revealed that there was a power within him *which was not him.*

Few believers are aware that there is within each of us a power that pulls us toward sinful actions. The Bible says this power resides within our bodies (Romans 7:23). Yet that power is not who we are. This fact must be recognized if we want to experience victory.

When my son, Andrew, was 20 years old he fell at a construction site and broke his back. His injury required surgery. Imagine how things might have developed if the surgeon had accidentally left a sponge inside him when they closed him up after performing the operation. A few days after the surgery, the conversation might have gone like this when the physician entered Andrew's hospital room for a follow-up visit.

"How are you feeling now, young man?"

"Doc, I believe there is something seriously wrong with me."

"Why do you think something is wrong with you?" the doctor asks.

"Well, there are several reasons. First, ever since the operation I have had an insatiable thirst. I can't get enough water to drink! And Doc, there's another thing, too. I haven't emptied my bladder since I came out of the operating room."

"Hmm, we'll need to run some tests to see what the problem is," the doctor says. "Nurse, schedule this patient for x-rays immediately."

A few hours later the doctor returns. He sheepishly walks over to the bed. "Son, I have found the source of your problem. There is nothing wrong *with* you; there is something wrong *in* you!"

This silly illustration demonstrates the exact way that a Christian is related to indwelling sin. For many years, I believed that I must actually be an evil man inwardly. I had a great desire to glorify God, yet I saw what I thought was another side of me. I believed that I had an "evil twin" living within me who wanted to have control of my lifestyle. Consequently, I often prayed for God to help me so that the part of me which was evil would be subdued. I worked hard to suppress what I believed to be the evil part of me. Paul, however, made a strong distinction between himself and the sin that was within him.

> If I do the very thing I do not wish to do, I agree with the Law, confessing that it is good. So now, no longer am I the one doing it, but sin which indwells me. For I know that nothing good dwells in me, that is, in my flesh; for the wishing is present in me, but the doing of the good is not. For the good that I wish, I do not do; but I practice the very evil that I do not wish. But if I am doing the very thing I do not wish, I am no longer the one doing it, but sin which dwells in me (Romans 7:16-20).

Does this sound like the confession of an evil man? Does it sound like a man who loves sin? Paul said that he was doing the thing that he did not wish to do. He said that the wishing to do good was always present in him, despite the fact that his actions might at times indicate otherwise. Does this predicament resemble your own experience? You may have assumed that you are a bad person simply because you recognize something within you pulling you toward sin. That inclination within you, however, is not you! It is *in* you, but it is not *you*. Paul continues:

I find then the principle that evil is present in me, the one who wishes to do good. For I joyfully concur with the law of God in the inner man, but I see a different law in the members of my body, waging war against the law of my mind, and making me a prisoner of the law of sin which is in my members (7:21-23).

What a discovery to realize that the Christian is not evil! There is something evil *within* the Christian, but he himself is not evil. Paul described our situation perfectly, saying, "I find then the principle that evil *is present in me*, the one who wishes to do good." He recognized the distinction between the power of sin and his own identity. He did not see himself as an evil man, but recognized that evil was present in him.

The Key to Victory

We take an essential step toward victory when we understand that we are not our own enemy. The enemy is the power of sin, which is in our body. Once we make the distinction between ourselves and indwelling sin, then we are in a position to take the next step toward victory. This step involves answering an important question raised by the apostle Paul.

Paul presents the definitive question regarding sin in Romans 7:24 when he asks, "Who will set me free from the body of this death?" Overcoming our sin involves asking the right question. For 29 years after I became a Christian, I asked all the wrong questions. The wrong questions will never lead to a right answer! Concerning my sins, I sometimes asked, "*What* can I do to experience victory?" At other times, I prayed, "Lord, *how* can I overcome my sins?" Paul didn't ask such questions. He recognized that the key to victory doesn't come by asking *what* or *how*. The key to victory over sin is a *Who!* Asking *what* or *how* suggests that there must be a plan or method that can enable a person to overcome sin. God's provision for our sins is not a plan, but the Person of Jesus Christ.

Soaring with Jesus

The principle of indwelling sin is a reality in the life of every believer. As long as we live in our physical body, it will be a force with which we must reckon. God has given us, however, the antidote for the power of sin through Jesus Christ. After his lengthy discourse on the problem in Romans 7, Paul sets forth this truth with clarity in chapter eight, verse two: "For the law of the Spirit of life in Christ Jesus has set you free from the law of sin and of death."

 At every moment that we depend totally on Him to express His life through us, we will experience victory over sin.

The law of sin and death is always present, seeking to pull the Christian down into independent living at every moment, but there is another law in which the Christian may rest. It is the law of the Spirit of life in Christ Jesus. The latter law will always supersede the former. As we trust Him, Jesus will never fail to overcome the law of sin and death.

Imagine being told that a man jumped off the Empire State Building in New York City. What image comes to your mind? You may ask many questions about that incident, but one thing that you would never ask is, "Did he fall?" You would assume the man fell because of your understanding of the law of gravity. It is a universal law that affects everyone.

What if you then were told that the man who jumped had been holding onto a hang glider? Your mental picture immediately changes because of your understanding of another law—the law of aerodynamics. With the added information, you wouldn't envision the man falling, but instead you would see him soaring over the skyline of New York. While you recognize the law of gravity, you also understand that, in a situation like this, the law of aerodynamics would overcome the law of gravity.

Does the law of gravity cease to exist while the man is soaring with the hang glider? Not at all, but the man is resting in a higher law. So it is with the believer. While the power of sin always resides within the Christian, the law of sin and death is not able to find its expression as long as the believer rests in the sufficiency of Christ. At every moment that we depend totally on Him to express His life through us, we will experience victory over sin.

What would happen if the man with the hang glider decided that he wanted to function independently of it? At the exact moment that he decided to do so, the law of gravity would once again become operative and he would immediately fall. If he chose to separate himself from the hang glider, nobody would be surprised that he fell. In fact, they wouldn't expect anything otherwise.

When a Christian abides in Christ, depending on Him as his life source at every moment, he will experience victory over sin. However, at any moment that a believer decides to function apart from Jesus, he will sin. There is no other possibility for him. There is no middle ground. Either a Christian chooses to depend entirely on Christ or else he doesn't. When our lifestyle is absorbed into our intimacy with Him, victory is the natural expression of His life within us. We soar above the downward pull of indwelling sin because we are carried along by the gentle breeze of His love.

The Christian will never be free from the presence of sin as long as we live in the physical bodies we now possess. But when grace rules in a believer's life, he will find freedom from the power of sin. God, of course, will allow us to play in the dirt with our sins if that is what we choose to do. However, I want to encourage you to look up from your sins and check out the One beside you. When you see His glorious beauty and hear His enticing voice, don't be surprised if you find yourself wanting to leave your sins and go follow Him. After that, why would you ever want to look back?

• • •

Dear Father,

You know all the sins in my life. Thank You for showing me that I hate those sins, even when I have found pleasure in them. I acknowledge that my sins do not reflect who I truly am. From this point forward, I choose to set my mind on You, not my sins. Lord Jesus, I can't deliver myself from my sins. I am trusting You to cause me to experience victory over sin's power. May I learn to receive Your love so that I may be so caught up in intimacy with You that my sins simply fall away. I trust You to enable me to experience the freedom You provide.

G.R.A.C.E. Group Questions

1. Read Colossians 3:1-3. How does setting our mind on Christ enable us to find freedom over sin's power? Discuss how this passage relates to what Paul had to say in Romans 8 about setting our mind on the things of the flesh.

2. What were the two lies that Jim believed which kept him enslaved to pornography? List some other common lies that the enemy uses to keep a Christian from experiencing freedom over sins. Identify a specific lie which you have believed about your own sins.

3. Discuss the meaning of indwelling sin. What verses prove that the power of sin is not a part of the Christian's identity? Paraphrase Romans 7:16-20 in your own words.

4. What are some common methods that Christians utilize in an effort to overcome personal sins? Explain the meaning of Romans 7:24-25.

5. What is the law of sin and death? What is the law of the Spirit of life in Christ Jesus? How does a Christian experience the law of the Spirit of life in Christ Jesus?

6. How would you relate to a Christian friend who is living in open sin? What would you say to this person? What verses would you show him to help him find freedom through Christ?

7

Knowing God's Will

*P*RAY FOR ME TO KNOW God's will," Brent said. "I have three job offers and I'm not sure which one I'm supposed to accept. I don't want to miss God's perfect will by taking a job I'm not supposed to have," he continued. "Please pray that the right choice will become very clear to me *soon.*"

Brent was a close friend of mine and I knew that he had a sincere desire to glorify God in the decisions he made in his life. Yet I could see that he was experiencing real anxiety over which choice to make in this matter. He had been without a job for almost three months, but now he had three offers, all coming within days of each other. The irony of the situation was that he had seemed more relaxed during the months that he had no job offers than he did when he had three. Any of the three sounded good to me, but his concern over picking the right option made him tense.

Brent needed to understand how to apply grace to the decision-making process. When grace rules a person's life, his perspective changes on everything. He begins to understand that every detail of life flows from his relationship with God. Grace means that God does it all. We simply receive from Him, cooperating with the Holy Spirit by trusting Him moment by moment. To walk in grace doesn't mean that we are passive in matters of daily living. To the contrary, it means that we act in confidence, resting in the fact that it is God who will initiate, perpetuate, and consummate His plan for our lives.

Many believers fall short of the joy God intends for them because they fail to understand how His grace acts on our behalf to bring to pass the wonderful plan He has for us. God has an awesome plan for your life. It isn't a cookie-cutter plan, either. He designed a special agenda that was uniquely created just for you. Before you were ever born, He saw you and customized His plan for your lifetime. One of the greatest joys in life is knowing that you are experiencing the very purpose for which you were created. Fulfilling the will of God is not some elusive goal that can never be reached. It is possible for Christians to enjoy the experience of *knowing* that we are in the very center of God's purpose.

Changing Our Perspective

Do you want to experience the joy of confidently knowing and doing the will of God? Then it is important to understand the difference between a legalistic approach to God's will and resting in Him through the grace walk. To a legalist the will of God is all about *doing.* He believes that it is his responsibility to find and fulfill God's specific plan for him. He is often sincere, yet his perspective actually cheats him out of the greatest benefit associated with God's will. The greatest blessing in experiencing God's will is the joy of experiencing God Himself! Yet the legalist is so focused on making the right choice that he usually misses the intimacy God intends for him to enjoy. This Christian believes that he has a job to do for God. Because of his drive to *do something*, he often makes a better church member than Christian. He *can* often accomplish many good things. The only problem with the things he does is that God is nowhere to be found in his activity. That is a serious problem.

The Will of God Is Jesus

The starting point for understanding the will of God must be grace. Remember that legalism is the method of living whereby we try to make spiritual progress based on what we do. The legalist asks, "*What* is the will of God for me?" Yet before we can correctly relate to the *what* of God's will, we must properly relate to the *Who* of His will. The will of God is not primarily a plan, but instead is a Person. Jesus Christ is the will of God. When one rightly relates to Him, doing the will of God becomes the natural result of our union with Him.

Many Christians live like deists. A deist basically believes that God created the world, fueled it up like a car, and then stepped back to watch it run its course. Deism recognizes very little personal interaction between God and His world. Its perspective implies that God has empowered the car (earth) to run, and now it is up to man where he drives it. Of course, most Christians would contest such a view. We believe that God is very much involved in the detailed events of this world. Yet many Christians act like a deist when it comes to God's will. They look for God to show them His will so that they can then go out and do it.

In his book *Experiencing God,* Henry Blackaby uses a great illustration to demonstrate how God purposes to accomplish His will within us. He suggests that there are two ways a person can reach a destination to which he has never been. He can ask directions from a friend who has been there. That friend can draw him a map that clearly shows how to reach the destination. That method may work, assuming the driver knows how to read a map. However, there is a second way which would absolutely guarantee that the driver would reach his desired destination. Instead of asking for a map, he could ask his friend to get into the car with him and direct him as they drove. In that way the friend would *become* the map.

---

*A person ruled by law
will pursue God's will with sincerity
and yet never be confident that he has
discovered it. One who enjoys intimacy
with Jesus will know it without
struggling to find it.*

That's a perfect description of how Jesus fulfills the will of God in us. When we understand our union with Him, he *becomes* the will of God to us, expressing His life through us so that every detail of God's will is fulfilled in our lifestyles. Jesus is the One who can cause us to know and do the will of God. Apart from Him, there is no way for one to experience the will of the Father. Paul said, "It is God who is at work in you, both to will and to work for His good pleasure" (Philippians 2:13). God the Holy Spirit within us will fulfill the Father's plan as we are absorbed into a continuous awareness of our oneness with Christ. To be more accurate with the illustration,

Jesus isn't just our map—He is the driver, the car, and the road. He is everything to us!

What Are You Seeking?

The goal of seeking to know God's will is a noble one if properly understood. A clear understanding will draw the Christian toward Jesus Christ. When grace rules our decision-making process, our focus will be on Him, not a plan.

The propensity toward seeking the right path presents another subtle danger. It places the responsibility on us to figure out God's will. Where grace rules, man is the recipient of good things and God is the Giver. So under grace, it isn't the Christian's duty to *find* God's will, but rather God will *reveal* His will to the one who rests in Him. A person ruled by law will pursue God's will with sincerity and yet never be confident that he has discovered it. One who enjoys intimacy with Jesus will know it without struggling to find it.

A biblical model for knowing the will of God is presented in Acts 13, where Paul and Barnabas were sent out on a missionary journey by the church at Antioch. How did this church know who to send out as their very first missionaries? There was no missions committee meeting in which key leaders decided that the church needed to begin a missions program. How did these early Christians know the will of God concerning the great missionary, Paul? Luke records how it happened:

> Now there were at Antioch, in the church that was there, prophets and teachers: Barnabas, and Simeon who was called Niger, and Lucius of Cyrene, and Manaen who had been brought up with Herod the tetrarch, and Saul.

And while they were ministering to the Lord
and fasting, the Holy Spirit said, "Set apart for
Me Barnabas and Saul for the work to which I
have called them. Then, when they had fasted
and prayed and laid their hands on them, they
sent them away (Acts 13:1-3).

The key to their understanding of God's will is that it
was revealed to them "while they were ministering to the
Lord and fasting." These saints were not merely seeking to
know the *will* of God; they were seeking *God* and He
spoke clearly to them, making His will clearly known.
They discovered the *plan* while they were seeking the
Person of God.

While legalism insists that we find the will of God,
God's grace causes Him to speak to us concerning His will
as we experience intimate interaction with Him. Legalism
puts the burden on the Christian to listen hard enough to
hear God's will. A Christian ruled by grace knows that
God is quite capable of speaking loudly enough to be
heard!

Imagine me coming into the room where my teenage
son is watching television. "David, I want you to mow the
lawn," I might say. He doesn't respond. He is mesmerized
by the program he is watching.

"David, did you hear me? I want you to mow the
lawn," I repeat. Still no response.

"David!" I say louder. "Yes sir?" he finally answers. "I
want you to mow the lawn." "Okay, dad."

Am I angry with my son because he honestly didn't
hear me? Of course not. I wouldn't scold him, saying,
"Whenever you are watching television, you had better
keep one ear open to me in case I want something from

you!" I know that in that instance, the burden of communication is on me.

That's how it is with God. He is our heavenly Father and it is His responsibility to cause us to hear when He speaks. You don't have to worry about missing God's will because you weren't listening carefully enough. When you abide in Christ, He assumes the responsibility of causing you to hear.

What are you seeking? What good would it do a Christian to discover the plan God had for him if he were not experiencing the intimate union of being joined to Jesus Christ? By what power can we fulfill His purpose apart from Him? Given numerous options, does it matter which one we choose if we then seek to carry out the plan by our own strengths and abilities? Even if we knew the right plan, it would be pointless to seek to do God's will apart from intimate dependence upon Him. When we live in total dependence upon Him, His will will be revealed with absolutely no struggle on our part. That's how to experience God's will through grace!

Cooperating with the Spirit

While it is God's responsibility to reveal His will and not ours to find it, that doesn't mean that the believer is oblivious to the process by which He makes His will known. Don't misinterpret the fact that Christians are free from struggling to know God's will to mean that we are passive in the process. The Bible clearly teaches how we may cooperate with God in such a way as to expedite the revelation of His plans for us. There is a way to *prove* the will of God in our lives.

I urge you therefore, brethren, by the mer-
cies of God, to present your bodies a living and
holy sacrifice, acceptable to God, which is your
spiritual service of worship. And do not be
conformed to this world, but be transformed
by the renewing of your mind, that you may
prove what the will of God is, that which is
good and acceptable and perfect (Romans
12:1-3).

The apostle Paul suggests that there is a way to prove
the will of God in our life. It isn't necessary for us to
wander through life wondering whether or not we are in
God's will. Our cooperation with the Holy Spirit and obedience to God's Word will guarantee that we find His will
in a way that proves to be "good and acceptable and perfect."

Being a Living Sacrifice

Paul indicates that our first response to God in discovering His will is to yield ourselves to Him as a "living
and holy sacrifice." Every Jew in Rome who read these
words knew exactly what Paul was referring to when he
used that phrase. After Abraham's son, Isaac, was finally
born, God told Abraham to take his only son and offer
him as a sacrifice on a mountain in Moriah. Genesis 22:1-
14 tells the story of how Isaac was taken to the mountain,
bound, and laid on an altar to be destroyed by the knife in
his own father's hand. While Isaac certainly must have
been frightened when he realized his father's intent, there
is no evidence in the narrative that he struggled against
Abraham. His dad was an old man who easily could have
been overcome. Yet it appears that Isaac yielded to his
father's will, allowing himself to be bound and laid out for

the sacrifice. It was only when an angel of the Lord stopped Abraham that Isaac realized he wasn't going to die.

Paul says that in order to prove the will of God in our lives, we must become like Isaac. We must totally surrender ourselves to God, yielding to His purpose regardless of what it may be. Absolute abandon to God is the foundation in knowing His will. Presenting ourselves as a living sacrifice means that we take our hands off our own life and totally yield to Him. Absolute surrender brings an attitude of trust in Him with no conditions or strings attached. It is an affirmation that we will trust God and yield to Him, just as Isaac yielded to Abraham.

The only way to be free to experience God's will is to go through life with a loose grip on everything around us.

For months, Walt had lived with a nagging fear that he was about to lose his job. Rumors were circulating that his company was downsizing and that his department would suffer the most cutbacks. He had spent two months frantically looking for another job, to no avail. "I don't know what I'm going to do if I lose this job. You know that my wife is a homemaker, and we don't have much in our savings account. We will be in serious trouble if my job is phased out."

What would you tell Walt? Would you try to encourage him by assuring him that God would make sure that he didn't lose his job? That would be a mistake. Christians will have times when they find themselves unemployed, just like anybody else. Would you console him by telling him that he would definitely find a new job before he lost his current one? In reality, that might not happen either. Walt's need is to totally surrender his job situation to God. Right now he is holding onto the *right* to have a job. Whenever a person holds onto personal rights, he sets himself up for the tyranny of fear when those rights are threatened. The only way to be free to experience God's will is to go through life with a loose grip on everything around us. He is the only security we have in life—and He is enough!

When we totally abandon ourselves to God, we bring ourselves to a place where we can experience the unfolding of His plan in ways that we never could have imagined. It is sometimes scary to release our grip on our own life in order to experience His life, but it is the only way to know and do His will!

I didn't encourage Walt about his employment at all. I did explain to him that the things we fear will control us. I encouraged him to pray a prayer of absolute surrender to God, voluntarily giving up the right to his job. I advised him to continually acknowledge that God was his source of supply, not his employer. Only by choosing to be a living sacrifice was he able to overcome the fear that enslaved him.

In 1995, when it became apparent to our family that God was calling us out of the pastorate and into an itinerant ministry, Melanie and I faced some real fears. We had just built a new home that we were enjoying. Now God was leading us away from the apparent security of my predictable salary as a pastor to a place where we would be required to live totally by faith, trusting Him to provide our income. Imaginary voices began to whisper in our minds about all the things that could go wrong if we followed what we believed was God's plan for us. The possibility of falling behind on our house payments and ultimately losing our home was a nagging thought for us both. Would such a step of faith prove to be our financial undoing? We were scared.

Soon our fear revealed to us that we were holding onto the right to own the house we had built. We knew that the only way to be free of that fear was to completely surrender ourselves to Him. So one Friday we spent the night at a nearby mountain lodge so that we could be alone and face our fears. While we were there, we listed an inventory of the things we have in this world. We also wrote down every fear that came to our minds. We identified all the painful things that could happen as a result of our obedience to God in resigning the pastorate. Then we took our list and together prayed our way down the items we had identified. We gave up the right to stay in our house—in fact, we *gave* the house to God that night. We acknowledged every right we were holding onto which the Lord had shown us and we relinquished those rights. We left that place the next day totally free.

Today we don't worry about losing our house. We can't lose our house now because we have already lost it. No, the mortgage company hasn't foreclosed on the property. In fact, we've never been late with a mortgage payment. We lost it that night on the mountain when we gave it to God. He still lets us live in it, but we don't fear losing it now because it isn't ours to lose.

Being a Holy Sacrifice

To cooperate with the Holy Spirit so that we can know God's will means total abandon as a *living* sacrifice. Yet Paul added that we are to present ourselves as a *holy* sacrifice too.

This aspect of surrender is generally misunderstood by a legalist. He believes it is his responsibility to make himself holy through disciplined devotion and religious regiment. When grace rules, however, a person understands that there is nothing he can do to make himself holy. Nor is there a need for such because the Christian has been granted holiness as a gift in the person of Christ. Unless a believer understands that he has been made holy through his union with Jesus Christ, he will never enjoy the will of God because of his focus on himself.

> *Both life and holiness in the Christian come from the same source— Jesus Christ! We aren't to strive for either, but simply believe His Word and receive what He has given us.*

The same phrase in Scripture teaches that we are to be a *living* and *holy* sacrifice. You will never hear anyone suggest that the Christian should try to be more alive when he presents himself to God. We all know that we are totally alive already. Yet many believe that they should be more holy in order to present themselves to God. However, both life and holiness in the Christian come from the same source—Jesus Christ! He is our life. He is our holiness. We aren't to strive for either, but simply believe His Word and receive what He has given us. Paul said:

> By His doing you are in Christ Jesus, who became to us wisdom from God, and *righteousness* and sanctification, and redemption, that, just as it is written, "Let him who boasts, boast in the Lord" (1 Corinthians 1:30-31, emphasis added).

Jesus has become our righteousness; therefore, the biblical instruction to present ourselves as a holy sacrifice simply involves acknowledging who we are in Him as we yield ourselves to the Father. When a Christian recognizes that he possesses the righteous nature of Jesus, he will be able to receive the revelation of God's will for him without interference from the mistaken notion that he must first improve himself before he can be totally yielded to God.

Doing the Will of God

"Pray for me. I have a major decision to make and I don't want to get out of God's will," Marie explained. "You know Satan is really deceptive and I don't want to be deceived. Pray that God will protect me from a mistake. I don't want God's second best. Pray that I'll make the right choice."

Although sincere, Marie's prayer request bordered on a worship service in Satan's honor. Her request is typical of the approach taken by many Christians who seek to know and do God's will. Note how she expressed confidence in Satan's ability to deceive and mislead her. She was afraid that she would unintentionally stumble out of God's will. She was giving far more credit to the enemy than he deserves. By contrast, when grace rules your decisions, you will rest in the confidence that God is "able to keep you from stumbling" (Jude 24).

An understanding that Jesus Christ is God's will personified sets the Christian free from anxiety about missing His will. If you are abiding in Christ, trusting Him to animate your actions, you can move forward in faith, not fear. When Jesus Christ expresses His life through us, it is impossible to get out of the will of God! If believers gave as much credit to the ability of the Holy

Spirit to guide us into God's will as many give to Satan's ability to lead us out of God's will, freedom would reign in the church.

Have you found yourself verbally expressing your faith in Satan's ability to deceive you? If so, stop it. Just relax and trust Jesus! If He is expressing His thoughts and actions through you, there is no reason for anxiety. In His grace, God gently guides us into His plans for our lives and all of hell can't stop that! Nobody has ever said it better than King Nebuchadnezzar. In Daniel 4:35 he confessed, "[God] does according to His will in the host of heaven and among the inhabitants of the earth; and no one can ward off His hand, or say to Him, 'What hast Thou done?'" *God will do whatever He wants to do!*

We don't need to agonize over the will of God. If knowing and doing the will of God depends on our own strength and ability, then we have no hope. But it isn't up to us! Jesus will fight every battle to guarantee that we accomplish the will of His Father. Four hundred years ago, Martin Luther rightly said:

> Did we in our own strength confide, Our
> striving would be losing,
> Were not the right Man on our side, The Man
> of God's own choosing:
> Dost ask who that may be? Christ Jesus, it is
> He;
> Lord Sabaoth His name, From age to age the
> same,
> And He must win the battle.

When we walk in grace we can trust that Jesus is directing our thoughts, and allowing us to act boldly. God does at times speak to his children in sensational and mystical ways, but much of the time He speaks to us through our thoughts. It is exciting when God speaks clearly in ways that leave little room for doubt, but usually He speaks and reveals His will without the help of electrifying phenomena.

> *While I'm completely responsible for how I handle my thought life it is not a sin to hear an ungodly thought in my mind.*

The apostle Paul often received visions and even heard God speak audibly at least once. Yet he never sought such experiences. He trusted the Holy Spirit within him to fulfill God's will. He trusted his own thoughts, declaring on one occasion, "We have the mind of Christ" (1 Corinthians 2:16). Paul didn't agonize over knowing the will of God—he just *did* it! He trusted that his thoughts were actually the thoughts of Christ within him.

Whose Thoughts Are These?

Often I am asked, "How do I know if my thoughts are coming from God, Satan, or myself?" That's an important question for someone who wants to know God's will. If we are going to take the advice we hear in our minds, we should know where our thoughts originate.

Thoughts from the Enemy—These thoughts are easy to identify. Anything that contradicts the righteous character of God or violates His Word comes from our adversary. Christians are godly people who "have the mind of Christ," so it's obvious that unholy thoughts don't originate with us. Holy people don't produce unholy thoughts.

Yet we sometimes *hear* unholy thoughts. Why? Not every thought you have is your own. When an unholy thought comes into your mind, you can be assured that it didn't originate there. It was introduced from outside.

It is helpful to know that the enemy introduces thoughts into the minds of Christians. I remember times when, while I was praying, a horrible thought suddenly came into my mind. Have you had that experience? I'd be praying, and unexpectedly a horrible word would pop into my head, seemingly out of nowhere. Then I would say, "Oh God! Forgive me! How could I think about that—especially while I'm praying?" It was such a dirty trick; Satan would introduce a thought to me and then condemn me for having it! Later I found freedom when I realized that while I'm completely responsible for how I handle my thought life, it is not a sin to *hear* an ungodly thought in my mind.

I was once counseling a man who battled with this problem. Periodically, blasphemous thoughts would cross his mind. This led him to believe that he had committed the unpardonable sin. Yet the man was a Christian. I attempted to explain to him that not all his thoughts were his own, but he didn't understand.

There was another person in the room with us observing our meeting. I leaned toward the man with the problem and motioned for him to lean toward me. I then whispered in his ear, "Do you see Jim sitting there beside you?" He nodded.

"Slap him in the face as hard as you can," I said. The man looked at Jim and then looked at me, bewildered. I waited. He sat there for a moment, looking back and forth. Again I motioned for him to lean toward me, then whispered, "With an open hand, slap Jim in the face so hard that you knock him off the chair!" (Jim didn't know his vulnerable position at this moment!) Then I sat back. The man looked confused, unsure of what to do.

Finally, I asked him aloud, "Are you going to do it?" "No!" he answered. "Well, are you at least going to confess to God that you had such a terrible thought?" I asked. "No," he said. "Why not?" I persisted. "Because *you* said it!" he responded. "That's right," I said. "And somebody else is saying things to you sometimes, too, but you've been taking the blame for it."

Again, it's important to recognize that there is no sin in the *awareness* of a thought. The Christian is responsible only for what he *does* with that thought. In 2 Corinthians 10:5, Paul tells exactly how he dealt with such thoughts: "We are destroying speculations and every lofty thing raised up against the knowledge of God, and we are taking every thought captive to the obedience of Christ." The believer's defense against evil thoughts is Jesus!

Thoughts from God or Ourselves—What if the thought that comes to mind doesn't contradict the nature of God's holiness? Is it my thought, or God's? The answer is "yes"— it is *our* thought. When we abide in Christ, we can trust that our thoughts are the thoughts of Jesus. Remember, we have the mind of Christ. That does not suggest that we *are* Jesus Christ or that we lose our distinct individuality when we abide in Him. What it does mean is that Jesus will express His thoughts and actions through our own individual personality, thus fulfilling the will of God in us.

A Christian abiding in Christ can trust his thoughts and act decisively in life. The fact that you may have doubts doesn't mean that you aren't acting in faith. If there is no room for doubt in your decision, then there is no *need* for faith. To experience God's will, a Christian simply needs to abide in Christ, then act in boldness. The rest is up to God.

Does this suggest that our ability to make choices is infallible? Not at all. Yet the potential for making a mistake should never paralyze us from making decisions. As we depend on the indwelling Holy Spirit to guide us, He will intervene at any point where we might unintentionally go astray. He can be trusted to stop us from making the wrong choice.

~ *Although it may have seemed that a mistake had happened that was out of God's will, Jesus was in God's will as He hung on the cross.*

On at least one occasion Paul found himself at a place where he might have made a wrong choice if the Holy Spirit had not shown him that his intentions were out of line. During Paul and Barnabas's second missionary journey, after they visited Mysia, they decided to move on to their next destination. Luke wrote: "When they had come to Mysia, they were trying to go into Bithynia, and *the spirit of Jesus did not permit them*" (Acts 16:7, emphasis added). How wonderful to know that Jesus within us will *keep* us in the perfect will of the Father!

Knowing that Jesus is expressing His thoughts and actions through you as you abide in Him will set you free from fear. If you are depending totally upon Christ to lead you, He will do it! If you start to make a mistake, He won't permit it. A lack of understanding in this area will cause a person to move forward in a tentative, almost paranoid manner. Knowing that the Spirit of Jesus will keep us in

His will enables the Christian to move forward with enthusiasm, joy, and anticipation. The God who saved you will also guide you! Don't worry about going astray. Simply choose to depend entirely upon Him to guide your steps, then move out in faith.

I Really Thought This Was God's Will

If Satan can't paralyze us with fear about moving forward in God's will, he will try to make us think that we have missed it. For example, a pastor friend of mine, David, came to me one day and said, "Steve, I really believed that God was leading me to pastor this church when I came. But the way things have turned out, I think I might have missed God's will on this one."

David's concerns arose because after just a few short months, things weren't moving along in the church as he had expected. In addition, some of the key leaders in the church were already criticizing him. This scared him. "A guy usually gets a short honeymoon in the church before this kind of stuff starts," he said.

David's fear that he had missed God's plan for him is a common concern. Christians often make decisions with certain expectations about the results of their choice. When the results don't turn out the way they hoped, they may think that they have somehow gotten out of the will of God. This is a lie that will cause a person to become unproductive in spite of the fact that he is exactly where God wants him. When a person believes he is out of God's will, he will lose all motivation to act in confidence and faith.

Maybe you have made choices only to later wonder what went wrong. You prayed about the choices. You evaluated them and then made your decision. Then things turned sour. Does this mean you missed God's will? No. Psalm 37:23

says, "The steps of a man are established by the LORD." God *did* direct your steps. Does it make sense that you could have sincerely *prayed* and earnestly *trusted* God to guide you only to have Him idly sit by and watch you make a mistake? Our loving Father will *not* permit that to happen!

When events don't unfold in the way you want or expect, it simply means one thing: God has a different plan. You aren't out of His will, but are discovering that His will is producing results you didn't expect. A person may argue, "But this *can't* be from God! It's all wrong!" Don't try telling that to Daniel, who found himself in a lions' den after he acted in faith. Or to Paul, who found himself shipwrecked on the island of Malta and was bitten by a poisonous snake while there—*after* he determined to make his way to Rome to proclaim the gospel in the heart of the empire. John faithfully preached God's Word because he knew that was God's will for him. Consequently he found himself exiled on the isle of Patmos. These examples affirm that when it may *appear* that we are out of God's will, we are actually in the center of His perfect plan for us. *Never* second-guess God's will after you have acted in faith.

The disciples and others might have concluded that God's will wasn't behind the crucifixion of Jesus. Yet beyond the natural reality of a crucifixion on Friday was the coming supernatural reality of a resurrection on Sunday! Although it may have seemed that a mistake had happened that was out of God's will, Jesus was *in* God's will as He hung on the cross. Don't conclude otherwise about your life when you find yourself on a cross. *God is in control!* Honor Him by affirming that He has indeed directed your steps even when they led to a place that you did not expect.

Pick a Spot and Run!

Imagine yourself standing in the center of a large field with an unobstructed view of the horizon in every direction. To the west you can see the ocean. To the east you can see a beautiful mountain range. To the north is a lush wooded forest. Looking south, you see a beautiful lake shaded by overhanging trees. As you look, you see many small points on the horizon. Those points represent your choices in life. You can go to any one of them; many look interesting, others don't. Which points should you choose? If you are trusting Christ within you, the answer is easy. You can choose any place you desire. Of course, it's important that you are enjoying an intimate union with Jesus at the time you make your choice. In other words, don't act independently of Him. Trust Him to guide your thoughts, then make your decision!

Have you selected the point on the horizon to which you want to go? Then run! Run there as fast as you can. Run with excitement and joyful anticipation. When you reach the spot you have selected, do you know what you will find? Jesus will be standing there. You'll see His arms outstretched toward you, and He will be laughing with joy. "Come on!" He will say. "Run! Run! I've been waiting for you to get here! This is *exactly* where I wanted you to be!" "Lord!" you exclaim. "I'm so glad You're here! No matter what this place holds for me, I *know* the Father's purpose will be done because You drew me here and will be with me at every moment."

When grace rules your life, you'll experience the joy that comes from knowing and doing God's will. You don't have to be afraid; trust Jesus and go forward in faith. As you abide in Him, He will keep you in His will at every moment. He *is* God's will, and you are in Him.

You can't go wrong with that kind of arrangement!

• • •

Dear Father,

I haven't enjoyed full freedom in Christ because I haven't understood how to know and do Your will. Now I understand that Your will for me begins with my intimacy with Jesus—as I abide in Him, the specifics of Your plan will become clear. Teach me to trust You so that I make choices in faith, not fear. Enable me to move forward with confidence. I renounce the fears that have paralyzed me and I affirm that I am trusting You to guide my thoughts and desires. I ask You to keep me in Your will, and I praise You that You will do it.

G.R.A.C.E. GROUP QUESTIONS

1. Discuss the difference between a grace-oriented approach to decision-making and a legalistic approach. Paraphrase Philippians 2:13 in your own words. What would this verse say if it had been written by a legalist?

2. Read Acts 13:1-3. When it comes to knowing God's will, how does the church at Antioch compare with the modern church? In what ways does the modern church seek to *find* the will of God? Describe a specific time when God *revealed* His will to you.

3. In what ways can we cooperate with the Holy Spirit so that we can readily know God's will? Discuss what it means to be a "living and holy sacrifice" (Romans 12:1-2).

4. How does holding onto personal rights keep a person from knowing God's will? Discuss a time when you experienced fear because one of your rights was threatened. How was the matter resolved?

5. What would you tell a Christian who says he is afraid that Satan may deceive him, causing him to get out of God's will? What verses would you show him from the Bible?

6. How does a person know whether his thoughts are his own, from God, or from Satan?

7. Describe a time in your life when the Holy Spirit intervened and kept you from making a wrong choice. Also, think of a time when you thought you had made a wrong choice, but later discovered that God had led you all along.

8

A
Smiling God

J EREMY HAD COME to seek counseling because of personal problems in his family. "I tried God and all that religious stuff," he said. "It just didn't work for me, so I walked away from God."

"Describe God to me," I said. As Jeremy did so, I immediately understood why he had decided to walk away. The god of his imagination was nothing like the One presented in the pages of Scripture. His god was one whose personality more closely resembled a cruel prison warden than a loving Father.

After further discussion with Jeremy, I discovered that he wasn't a Christian. He had been reared in a religious home where attendance in a legalistic church was the extent of the spiritual input he received. Between his legalistic church and spiritually dead home, he developed a concept of God that would repulse anyone.

Jeremy struggled with a real dilemma. On one hand, he wanted no part of God as he understood Him to be. On the other, he couldn't satisfy the spiritual hunger that gnawed within him. While his mind rejected all things spiritual, his heart cried out for the fulfillment that can only be known through experiencing the life God offers.

Jeremy's hunger for God is a universal condition. Blaise Pascal, the French philosopher and physicist, wrote, "Within the heart of every man is a God-shaped void that cannot be filled by created things, but only by the Creator through His Son Jesus Christ." People will go to amazing lengths to fill that God-shaped void. If necessary, they will *create* a god in their attempt to satisfy their spiritual longings. This is affirmed by contemporary society's preoccupation with spirit beings, evolved spiritual entities, and a countless number of options from various world religions.

What ever happened to the God of the Bible? How tragic that so many modern Christians have a concept of God that is far removed from the truth! Many who grew up under the suffocating influence of a rules-based religion can't even begin to comprehend God as a Father who looks upon them with a smile. When a church's entire focus is on religious performance, it is next to impossible to see God clearly. It's easier to find the answer to "Where's Waldo?" than to see God in the middle of a church whose focus is entirely on religious performance.

The God I Invented

I was a young boy when I became a Christian. By the time I reached 16 years old, nobody could have been more sincere about their faith than I was about my walk with God. By the time I finished high school, I was as militant as a Christian soldier can be. I preached in parking lots at bowling alleys and movie theaters. I witnessed to anything that breathed. About the time I started college, I was introduced to the writings of men like E.M. Bounds, R.A. Torrey, Leonard Ravenhill, and others whose testimonies stirred my heart. I had a genuine desire to make my mark for God in this world.

When I was 19 years old, I became a pastor. Over the next few years, through nobody's fault but my own, my focus shifted. Gradually I found myself becoming more and more consumed with ministry and less and less with Jesus. I still loved the Lord, but I wasn't *in love* with Him the way I once had been. The work of ministry gradually became my life. I believed that God had called me to *do* something great for Him and I certainly didn't want to let Him down. In small, undetectable increments I moved away from the Christ-centered lifestyle I had enjoyed, and took on a service-oriented lifestyle.

Although I was as sincere as I had always been, a metamorphosis began to occur in my mind. In my perception, the God of my childhood who loved and accepted me unconditionally became a God whose attitude toward me was determined by how well I served Him. I imagined a God who was more like a divine Employer than a devoted Father. I believed that His blessings came as a result of my faithfulness. When circumstances were hard, I assumed that I was doing something wrong. I would examine my life, looking for deficiencies—which are always apparent when one is absorbed in critical self-examination. Consequently, I felt unacceptable before God because I had so far to go in overcoming my deficiencies as a Christian. The God I invented could never be totally pleased because I would never be totally perfect. He seldom smiled; in fact, He often appeared frustrated with me.

Recognizing God's Faithfulness

During that time, the fatal flaw in my misunderstanding of God was my emphasis on myself. I believed that *my* faithfulness caused God to bless me. But now that I understand the grace walk, I know that God's blessings aren't the result of my faithfulness, but because of His. God doesn't bless us because of how wonderful we are, but because of how wonderful He is!

The essence of legalism is the effort to gain God's blessings by what *we* do. This concept comes right out of an Old Testament mindset and shows no understanding of the covenant of grace. When Moses came down from Mount Sinai with the Law, he gave this message from God to the people of Israel: "Now then, if you will indeed obey My voice and keep My covenant, then you shall be My own possession among all the peoples" (Exodus 19:5). The prescription was clear—do the right thing, and you will be blessed. This method motivated the Jews to try hard to please God by their behavior. Yet in spite of all their efforts, they were always failing to be consistent in their devotion to God.

Grace is a system of living whereby God blesses us because we are in Jesus Christ, and for no other reason at all.

Back in chapter five, we saw that God didn't give the Law because He believed that the people would keep it. He gave them the law to prove that man *cannot* earn God's blessings—that he is incapable of consistently living a godly lifestyle on his own. Nobody is blessed by God because he deserves it. Every blessing finds its source in the grace of God. Grace is a system of living whereby God blesses us because we are in Jesus Christ, *and for no other reason at all.* Yet many Christians are miserable because they still live with an Old Testament perspective that causes them to try to stay in God's favor by good behavior.

Law demands, "Your behavior must improve to receive God's blessings!" Grace is the voice of God saying, "I will bless you until your behavior *does* improve!" When grace rules, a man *wants* to live a consistently godly lifestyle. It is the faithfulness of God that causes a person's heart to be changed so that he is motivated to godly living by desire, not duty. Remember what God said in Ezekiel 36:26-27:

> Moreover, I will give you a new heart and put a new spirit within you; and I will remove the heart of stone from your flesh and give you a heart of flesh. And I will put My Spirit within you and cause you to walk in My statutes, and you will be careful to observe My ordinances.

Three times in these verses God says, "I will." That's the meaning of grace. It's not about what we do, but about what God does as a result of His love for us. He promised that He would give His people a new heart (desires) and a new spirit (identity). He said that when His Spirit came into union with us, He would *cause* us to live a godly lifestyle. When grace rules, we experience *God's* faithfulness. The Christian life doesn't depend on our feeble efforts, but on His faithful empowerment within us! The real God is a faithful God who will accomplish what He has determined to do in us.

Receiving God's Forgiveness

Perhaps the one obstruction that most prevents people from seeing God's smiling face is a wrong view of God's forgiveness. Our God is a *forgiving* God toward all who are His. As a Christian, your sins are *all* forgiven. Forgiveness is the deliberate choice to release a person from all obligation he has toward us as a result of any offense he may have committed against us. God's decision to forgive you originated with a *choice*, and then was expressed through His own loving nature. You did nothing to deserve to be forgiven. He simply *chose* to forgive you. The choice was motivated by His character, not yours.

We owe God nothing for our sin. He chose to carry the weight of our offense against Him to the cross, and to release us from all obligation toward Him. Jesus satisfied God's demand for justice to be carried out, and the Father has chosen to totally release you from all debt to Him. You will never deserve God's forgiveness; you simply need to receive it and then walk in it!

Isn't God Angry When I Sin?

It isn't possible for a Christian to cause God to become angry. "There is nothing you can do that will make Him mad—nothing!" After making that statement to Peggy, she looked at me in disbelief.

"Are you saying that God feels no anger about sin?" she asked.

"Not about your sin," I answered. "When Jesus went to the cross, did He carry your sins with him?"

"Yes," she responded.

"How many of your sins were placed into Christ on the cross?" I continued.

"All of them," she replied.

"That's right. Then when Jesus said, 'It is finished,' didn't He mean that the penalty for *all* your sins had been paid?"

"Yes," Peggy said.

As our discussion continued, I showed Peggy where the Bible teaches that the Christian has received *total* forgiveness. When Jesus said, "It is finished," He was declaring that the penalty for our sin was paid in full. Every sin of our lifetime was dealt with at the cross. When you received Christ at salvation, you experienced total forgiveness, and God closed the book on your sins.

When Jesus died, God knew every sin you would ever commit. He poured out His scalding anger against your sin on Jesus, who became sin for you. Bearing the weight of our sins, and experiencing God's abandonment of Him, Christ cried out, "My God! My God! Why have You forsaken me?" God the Father had turned His back on His Son—because of *our* sins. In the agony of those hours, Jesus experienced in time the torment for sin that you would have experienced in eternity.

Centuries later, when the Holy Spirit drew you to Christ and you were born again, God poured out onto you the total forgiveness secured by Jesus at the cross. He doesn't ration it out a little at a time. Just as Jesus died for the sins of your whole lifetime, at the moment you were saved God granted you forgiveness for all the sins of your lifetime. *Believers stand before God in complete forgiveness.* You may be surprised by your sins and expect God to become angry, but your sins don't surprise Him. He has *already* been angry about those sins; so angry that He vented His rage against them at the cross. But it's over now. It's done! You are forgiven.

Asking for Forgiveness

When a Christian asks God for forgiveness of his sins, he implies that Jesus' work on the cross isn't finished even though Jesus clearly said that "it *is* finished." Some people, however, say that the New Testament teaches that Christians are to ask God for forgiveness when they sin. This is where it becomes important for us to "rightly divide the word."

> *Under law, if there is even one person whom you have not forgiven, then you can't be fully forgiven yourself.*

When did the new covenant of grace begin in the Bible? Many would say it started at the beginning of Matthew, yet the covenant did not actually start until the death of Jesus. The covenant of grace was the last will and testament of Jesus Christ. The age of grace could not become operative until Jesus died. The writer of Hebrews said:

> Where a covenant is, there must of necessity be the death of the one who made it. For a covenant is valid only when men are dead, for it is never in force while the one who made it lives (Hebrews 9:16-17).

Both Scripture and common knowledge demonstrate that a will does not become functional until the one who made it dies. Given that fact, which covenant was in operation during the whole lifetime of Jesus? Of course, it was the covenant of law. Jesus lived under the Old Testament covenant.

Remember that the purpose of the law is to raise the awareness of sin among those who embrace it. Living under the covenant of law, the words of Jesus often reflected that covenant. Such is the case when He discussed the matter of forgiveness. In Matthew 6:12, when Jesus responded to His disciples' inquiry about how to pray, He said this about forgiveness: "Forgive us our debts, as we also have forgiven our debtors." He elaborated on forgiveness under the law system in verses 14-15 by saying, "If you forgive men for their transgressions, your heavenly Father will also forgive you. But if you do not forgive men, then your Father will not forgive your transgressions." This was the law in action—if you want God to do something for you, then you must first do something to *cause* Him to act in your behalf. Under law, if there is even one person whom you have not forgiven, then you can't be fully forgiven yourself. If you aren't *fully* forgiven, you have no hope of heaven because one unforgiven sin is enough to keep you out.

When asked about forgiveness, Jesus answered according to the law. Yet in His personal relationships, he always acted in grace. An example of His approach is illustrated in John 8, where we read about the woman who was caught in the act of adultery. When the scribes and Pharisees pointed out that the law of Moses commanded that adulterers be stoned, Jesus didn't dispute the law. He simply suggested that their application of the law include themselves. After His challenge that the sinless one among them cast the first stone, the crowd dispersed until no one was left except the woman. Having acknowledged the validity of the law at that moment, Jesus went on to demonstrate gracious forgiveness toward the woman by asking, "'Woman, where are they? Did no one condemn you?' And she said, 'No one, Lord.' And Jesus said, 'Neither do I condemn you; go your way. From now on sin no more'"(verses 10-11). This incident is so typical of the Lord Jesus during His earthly ministry. He utilized the law to raise the awareness of sin and then demonstrated grace by His own behavior.

Under the covenant of law, a person was not totally forgiven yet had to receive ongoing forgiveness in order to remain in a guilt-free state. But at the cross, God poured out all His forgiveness toward those who are His. We don't need to ask for more forgiveness! Paul described total forgiveness in Colossians 2:13-14:

> When you were dead in your transgressions and the uncircumcision of your flesh, He made you alive together with Him, having forgiven us all our transgressions, having canceled out the certificate of debt consisting of decrees against us and which was hostile to us; and He has taken it out of the way, having nailed it to the cross.

When you appropriated God's forgiveness by trusting Christ, you were immediately acquitted for the sins of a lifetime! If you believe that your sins are still being forgiven one at a time as you commit them, a troubling question must be answered. What happens if you die with just one sin in your life which you haven't thought to ask Him to forgive? The truth of Scripture is that before we were born, God saw our lives and identified every sin that we would commit. Jesus carried all those sins to the cross with Him, and God canceled the debt. Every sin of our lifetime has been forgiven—past, present, and future! The real God is a forgiving God who never becomes angry with those who are His. The empty tomb put a smile on the face of God—a smile that has never gone away.

When grace rules, the Christian will see God as the One who has forgiven us for every sin of our lifetime!

Are you still living as if you were under the Old Testament by constantly asking for God's forgiveness? Those days are over and finished! Rejoice in the truth that you are totally forgiven. The old covenant is forever gone. The writer of Hebrews said:

> For if that first covenant had been faultless, there would have been no occasion sought for a second. For finding fault with them, He says,
>
> > "Behold, days are coming, says the LORD,
> > When I will effect a new covenant,
> > With the house of Israel and with the
> >   house of Judah;
> > Not like the covenant which I made with
> >   their fathers
> > On the day when I took them by the hand
> > To lead them out of the land of Egypt;
> > For they did not continue in My
> >   covenant,
> > And I did not care for them, says the
> >   LORD.
> > For this is the covenant that I will make
> >   with the house of Israel
> > After those days, says the LORD:

> I will put My laws into their minds,
> And I will write them upon their hearts.
> And I will be their God,
> And they shall be My people. And they
>   shall not teach everyone his fellow cit-
>   izen,
> And everyone his brother, saying, 'Know the
>   LORD,'
> For all shall know Me,
> From the least to the greatest of them.
> For I will be merciful to their iniquities,
> And I will remember their sins no more"
>   (Hebrews 8:7-12).

The day described in this passage is the day in which we live! When grace rules, the Christian will see God as the One who has forgiven us for every sin of our lifetime! The cross of Jesus was God's final word about our sins.

Resting in God's Favor

Until a Christian realizes that he has been totally for-given, he will never experience the freedom to enjoy min-istry to God and his fellow man. His faulty belief about forgiveness will necessitate that he constantly focus on himself, scrutinizing his every thought and action. In calling for the continuous habit of asking for forgiveness, legalism redirects the focus from God to self. Where law rules, one is preoccupied with his own behavior, while grace causes us to be preoccupied with Jesus.

I spent 29 years of my Christian life in self-examina-tion. I often asked for forgiveness for things I had done which I shouldn't have done as well as for things I didn't do which I should have done. Sometimes I even asked God to forgive me for sins I had committed that I didn't even know about. I wanted to cover all the bases. There's a word for that kind of lifestyle: bondage. When I came to realize God's total forgiveness of me, for the first time I was *free* to see His smiling face. Until then I stared at myself and imagined Him frowning.

Knowing God's Personality

Personality types have been categorized in as many ways as we can imagine. There are an abundance of personality tests that are supposed to help portray a person's temperament. Have you ever wondered what God's personality is like? How would you describe His personality? Some people might suggest that we can't know His personality, but that wouldn't be true. God has revealed Himself to us through His Son and His written Word. Stop reading and consider this question for a moment: *What if God is nothing like I have imagined Him to be?* Did you think about that for a moment? I asked you to pause because we only hurt ourselves when we hold onto any wrong perceptions about God. The sooner we have a right view of God, the more we'll see His smiling face. Are you willing to have your mind changed, if necessary, concerning what God is like? Consider the following descriptions of God's personality.

He Is a Loving and Laughing God

Christians serve a God who delights in them. The heart of the Lord is ecstatic about those who are His. Zephaniah 3:17 gives us a glimpse of God's exhilaration over us: "The LORD your God is in your midst, a victorious warrior. He will exult over you with joy, He will be quiet in His love, He will rejoice over you with shouts of joy." What an exciting thought! The God of the universe is so thrilled with you that He is overwhelmed with joy. Unable to contain His emotion, He shouts for joy when He looks at you.

You may not *feel* like God has such great admiration for you, but He does. In Ephesians 2:10, you are called God's workmanship. By placing you into Jesus Christ, God has made a beautiful new creation out of you. You deeply stir His divine passions. Nothing will ever change that fact.

Because you are a child of God, you can relax and enjoy Him. There is nothing you can do that would cause God to love you any more or any less than He does right now. You are His eternal bride in whom He finds great pleasure.

Do you know that you can relax and enjoy God's love without trying to earn it?

I met my wife when I was 16 years old. I have already described how excited I was about my first date with her. On the day of that date, I went to great effort to cause her to like me. As soon as I came home from school that Friday, I drove dad's car around into the backyard. I filled a pail with dishwashing detergent and went to work cleaning that car. I scrubbed it from top to bottom. I used tire black on the tires to make them shiny. I sprayed a special finish on the interior. I vacuumed the carpet. That car was *clean*.

About two hours before I was to pick her up, I began to get groomed and dressed. I showered and put on my navy blue pants, my light blue shirt, and even wore a tie. I wanted Melanie to like me! I soaked myself in cologne and drove to her house. I arrived early, so I circled the block until it was time to pick her up. When I pulled into her driveway, I checked my hair, sprayed breath freshener in my mouth, and sprinkled some more cologne on myself and on the side of the seat where she would be sitting. (I hoped it would get to her.) I walked up to the door and rang the doorbell. When her mother came to the door she invited me in, telling me that Melanie wasn't quite ready. "Oh, that's okay," I gushed. "I don't mind waiting at all!"

After a while Melanie walked into the room. I stood up and told her how beautiful she looked. As we walked to the car, I rushed ahead to open the door for her. I wanted her to like me. After the movie we went to eat. "Order anything on the menu," I said. "Do you want to get the large pizza with *all* the toppings? We can do that." I really wanted this girl to like me. She did.

Three years later I married her. The months passed. With time, my words and actions changed. I was saying, "You had better get in the car! I'm not going to be late for church again. I'll leave you. I mean it!" Then at the restaurant, "You know, we could just go to the drive-through at McDonalds. They'll sell those Happy Meals to adults!" I even let her open the car door for herself. I reasoned that I had her love now, so there was no need for all that "dating stuff" anymore.

Needless to say, by the end of our first year of marriage, conflict was common. Over a period of months as I prayed about our relationship, God revealed some things to me. I came to understand that I wasn't to serve my wife so that she would love me, but because it was a way to express my love for her. Soon I began to act differently toward her and our marriage changed. I've been opening the car door for her now for many years—not so that she will love me, but because I love her. I'm not obligated to serve her through considerate gestures now. I'm free to do those things because I can rest secure in her love for me.

Do you *know* that you can relax and enjoy God's love without trying to earn it? When we know how much God loves us, it frees us to serve Him out of gratitude and love for Him. God loves you whether or not you open the car door! Service is difficult if we are trying to earn His favor, but it becomes a pleasure when it is a natural expression of the intimate relationship we share with Him.

He Is an Accepting and Affirming God

Not only does God love you, but He also *likes* you. You don't need to improve for God to accept you. He saved you while you were still in the filth of your sins. Do you think that now He doesn't like you because you haven't reached perfection? "As high as the heavens are above the earth, so great is His lovingkindness toward those who fear Him" (Psalm 103:11).

Human beings often accept other people on the basis of qualities that they like. Sometimes we believe that God relates to us in the same way that we tend to relate to others. "You thought that I was just like you," God said in Psalm 50:21. But He isn't like us.

A man once went to an opera and heard a woman with a beautiful soprano voice. He was so mesmerized by her voice that he was convinced he had fallen in love with her on that very night. He went back to the opera house to hear her again the next night. Once again, his passions were stirred. The man continued to attend the opera every night for a week. Finally, he asked an usher if it would be possible to meet the singer in her dressing room after the show. When the singer agreed, it was arranged.

The man explained to her how he had come to hear her sing every night. He asked her to go out with him on a date. To his delight, she agreed. The two went out together after the performance each night for six weeks. He didn't really *know* her, but he was so captivated by her voice that he was convinced he loved her. At the end of six weeks, he proposed marriage, and she accepted.

A few days later they were married, then they left for their honeymoon. When they reached the hotel where they were to spend their first night together, they went to their room. The singer began to prepare to retire for the night. She reached up and pulled off a wig, revealing an almost bald head. She pulled false eyelashes off her barren eyelids. She pulled off her false fingernails. She took out her colored contact lenses. And last, she removed her false teeth. The man stood staring at her in shock. Finally he cried out, "Sing woman! Sing!"

That's the way people tend to be! But God isn't like a man. He has seen you with your hair off and your teeth out and He still adores you! He is absolutely accepting and always affirming because of His love for you. God knows your faults better than you know them. Still, He lovingly accepts and affirms you.

James Dobson tells the story of his late father, who had a dream shortly before his death. In the dream he saw Jesus sitting at a table, writing in a ledger. Mr. Dobson said that Jesus would write, look up at his father, smile, and then continue writing. Jesus repeated this sequence of actions several times, and Mr. Dobson became very curious about what Jesus was writing. So he stepped forward to get close enough to see what was being written.

Straining to see the ledger, he was finally able to read the words written by Jesus. They read, "For time and eternity, he is acceptable."

> *Imagine God looking at you. He is smiling, at times laughing out loud with joy. He adores you and it is obvious.*

How do you see God in your mind? Many Christians need to renew their minds with the truth concerning God's disposition. God isn't angry with those who are His. He isn't judgmental or punitive toward us. That was all finished at the cross. When you finish this chapter, put the book down for a moment and close your eyes. Imagine God looking at you. He is smiling, at times laughing out loud with joy. It is evident that the reason for His happiness is you! You can see the pride in His eyes. He *adores* you and it is obvious. One glimpse of His smiling face and you *know* that for time and eternity, *you are acceptable!*

• • •

Dear Father,

Open my eyes so that I can see You clearly. Tear down every false imagination I may have about what You are like. Cause me to understand how You really feel about me. I confess that I have judged You wrongly by failing to recognize and appreciate how much You love and accept me. Thank You for forgiving all my sins. Empower me to live in confidence and boldness, knowing that You are working on my behalf in every circumstance of life.

G.R.A.C.E. Group Questions

1. Jeremy decided to walk away from God because "it just didn't work" for him. His concept of God was partially formed by the input he received at a legalistic church. Describe what a legalistic church is like. What are the differences between a church built on legalism and one built on grace?

2. What would you say to a Christian who continues to struggle with guilt over past sins? What Bible verses would you show to this person? How does God feel about us when we sin?

3. Explain the difference between an old covenant and new covenant understanding of forgiveness. When did the new covenant begin? Why did Jesus tell His disciples that they would not be forgiven unless they forgave everybody who had offended them? Is that true for Christians today? Why or why not?

4. Read Colossians 2:13-14 and paraphrase the passage in your own words. How is it possible that God could forgive sins you haven't even committed yet? If future sins are already forgiven, what keeps Christians from living a lifestyle of continuous sins?

5. Describe the way you have imagined God to be. Has your understanding of God's personality changed any after reading this chapter? If so, how?

6. Read Zephaniah 3:17 in several different translations of the Bible. List three characteristics of God's character given in this verse.

7. Write a prayer to God acknowledging how *He* feels about you.

9
The
Complete Gospel

*I*MAGINE BEING a young adult so deep in debt that there is no way to become financially free in your lifetime. Envision, for as long as you live, always having bills larger than your paycheck. There is no way out. All you can do is hope to survive another month.

Then one day you receive an official-looking letter from a prestigious law firm. You open the letter and discover that a distant relative has died. The attorney is notifying you that in accordance with the terms of the will left by the deceased, all of your financial obligations have been paid in full. You no longer owe anything to anybody. Even your mortgage has been paid off. Can you imagine how excited you would be? You would probably talk about it constantly for weeks to anybody who would listen. After a while, although you would still be grateful, you wouldn't talk about the incident all the time anymore.

Over the next 30 years, you manage to do moderately well financially. You no longer experience poverty nor debt, but at the same time, neither have you enjoyed the luxuries of life. Your finances have provided an average lifestyle—nothing more and nothing less.

One day you receive a telephone call from someone who introduces himself as an investment advisor at a bank. "I wanted to discuss your account with you," he says. "I don't have an account at your bank," you say politely. He states your full name and asks, "Is that the person to whom I am speaking?" "Yes," you answer, "but I don't have an account there." He asks you to verify the address in his records. It is the address of your distant relative who died 30 years earlier. "That is the address to which we've been sending your statements all these years," he responds. As the conversation continues, you discover that the executor who took care of your rich relative's estate had opened an account in your name thirty years ago.

"How much is in the account?" you ask, curious.

"Brace yourself," says the banker. "The account has grown to several million dollars! Apparently the attorney who notified you about your debts being paid off failed to mention that you had also been left a very generous inheritance."

How would you feel upon receiving such news? For 30 years you lived a very modest lifestyle while, all along, you had the resources in the bank to live in the lap of luxury! You'd probably be wondering, *Why didn't that attorney tell me the complete story? Why did he fail to tell me about the wealth I inherited?*

The Whole Story

Every time I have thought back to the day when I was born again, I've felt gratitude that Jesus paid in full what I owed. Yet it was not until I had been a Christian for 29 years that I heard the complete story of salvation. I understood that the debt for my sin had been paid, but I didn't know the rich inheritance that was mine through the death of Jesus on the cross.

There is more to the New Testament gospel than many Christians realize. Somewhere over the past 20 centuries, the church has dropped the ball. We have done an excellent job of proclaiming the forgiveness available through Jesus Christ. However, we have fallen short in presenting the *complete* message of the gospel. We have often led people to believe that receiving forgiveness is the apex of the Christian faith. While receiving God's forgiveness is absolutely necessary, it isn't God's *ultimate* act in salvation.

Salvation is much more than being forgiven and going to heaven. Salvation is receiving divine life!

Jesus didn't come to earth and die just so we could be forgiven and go to heaven. If that is all there is to salvation, why does He leave us here on earth after we are saved? The pinnacle of salvation is not forgiveness, as necessary and wonderful as that may be. God forgave us for a reason. It is so that He can place His divine life *into* us and then express that life *through* us to the world *around* us. God cannot place His *Holy* Spirit into an unholy person. That's why forgiveness is essential. Once we have received His forgiveness, He gives us His *life*.

Jesus said in John 10:10 that He "came that they might have life." John 3:16 says that God sent Jesus so that whoever believes in Him would have "everlasting life." Do you get the picture? Salvation is receiving divine *life!* We have not declared the whole gospel when we stop at the place of forgiveness. The complete gospel makes it plain that God wants to take up residence in those who trust Him. He wants to move into a person and take over him completely. Salvation is much more than being forgiven and going to heaven. This limited understanding of what it means to be a Christian has produced a multitude of listless, lethargic Christians whose greatest spiritual ambition is to die and go on to heaven. So much for Christian soldiers marching on to war! Many live as if they're just killing *time* here while they wait to go to heaven. Somebody didn't tell them everything Jesus left in His last will and testament.

A Man with the Complete Message

The apostle Paul was consumed with a great desire to see people understand the *complete* gospel. He explains his calling in Colossians 1:25-28:

> Of this church I was made a minister according to the stewardship from God bestowed on me for your benefit, that I might *fully* carry out the preaching of the word of God, that is, the mystery which has been hidden from the past ages and generations; but has now been manifested to His saints, to whom God willed to make known what is the riches of the glory of this mystery among the Gentiles, which is Christ in you, the hope of glory. And we proclaim Him, admonishing every man and teaching every man with all

wisdom, that we may present every man *com-plete* in Christ (emphasis added).

Paul said that he wanted to *fully* preach the message God had given him. He wanted to proclaim the full Word of God—to leave nothing unspoken that needed to be declared. His goal was to present his converts *complete* in Christ.

What is this mystery Paul refers to in this passage? We can tell by the original Greek text and context that Paul wasn't talking about puzzling questions like those raised in a Sherlock Holmes story. The word refers to something that was not known before, but has now been unveiled and made plain. The mystery of grace is the realization of *Christ in you*. In the Old Testament, God came *upon* men, but did not dwell within them. Today, in the person of His Spirit, God comes *into* those who know Him. He becomes our very life by putting to death the person we were before salvation (Romans 6:6) and placing His divine nature into us (2 Peter 1:4).

Salvation has not come to complete fruition until one comes to understand the mysterious union that he shares with Christ. Partial evangelism leaves a person forgiven and going to heaven, but when grace rules a new convert, he understands that he is energized with divine life for today. Even a Christian legalist will share the message of forgiveness through the *death* of Jesus. But grace tells the whole story by offering dynamic power for living by the *life* of Jesus.

Although a Christian knows his sin debt has been paid, he will never fully experience the supernatural empowerment of God's life until he understands that Christ is not simply *in* his life; Christ *is* his life! The Christian's body is nothing less than a container for divine life. As we abide in Him, that life flows out of us continually.

Bud recently came to understand the implications of "Christ in you, the hope of glory." He realized that not only was he *totally* forgiven, but also that Jesus would express His life through him as he depended entirely on Him. "Steve, I've been thinking about it," he said. "Christ in me is sort of like the lead in a mechanical pencil. It's only doing what it was designed for when the lead is coming out of the pencil." That's it! The Christian is designed both to contain and release divine life so that we may make a mark on this world with the love of God. The Holy Spirit had revealed to Bud what Paul prayed that the Ephesian Christians would understand:

> I pray that the eyes of your heart may be enlightened, so that you may know what is the hope of His calling, what are the riches of the glory of His inheritance in the saints, and what is the surpassing greatness of His power toward us who believe (Ephesians 1:18-19).

A man understands the complete gospel when he knows the riches he has inherited by receiving the life of Jesus Christ. Some people have said, "When you have Jesus Christ, you have *everything* you need." That is exactly right, but what practical good does it do to have everything you need if you don't even know what you have? Many people don't understand how rich Christians are in Him.

Your Official Notification

In case you haven't already received the news, I want to notify you of something from which you may greatly benefit. This news offers you a brand new life, filled with privileges that are "exceeding abundantly beyond all that [you could possibly] ask or think" (Ephesians 3:20). If you act on the following information, your life will never be the same. There is nothing you must do to gain the benefits. The only condition is that you believe the message and receive the inheritance that has been left for you.

~ *Jesus left a last will and testament, outlining the riches He wants you to enjoy as your inheritance.*

You already know about the death of Jesus Christ on the cross. You understand that by His one-time payment, the debt for your sin has been paid in full. God poured out all His anger over your sin onto Jesus. By the shedding of His blood, your sins are forever gone.

That isn't the complete story, though. Jesus left a last will and testament, outlining the riches He wants you to enjoy as your inheritance. In this New Testament, your bequest is explained. This news may sound too good to be true, but you can believe it because these promises were made by God the Son, witnessed by God the Father, and will be implemented in your life by God the Holy Spirit. Consider these benefits you have inherited in Christ Jesus:

You Have a New Life

Have you ever wished you could be somebody else? Well, now you are! You aren't the same person you used to be before you became a Christian. You have been made into a brand new person (2 Corinthians 5:17) who has been created as one who is totally righteous (Ephesians 4:24). You are now holy (1 Corinthians 3:17), not because you did anything to deserve it, but because righteousness has been given to you as a gift (Romans 5:17). You still have the same body, but a new you lives inside! Christ is your life now (Colossians 3:4), and it is in Him that you live, and move around, and even exist (Acts 17:28).

Don't be deceived into believing this isn't true just because your behavior hasn't indicated it to be so. Your brain remembers the old man you were before salvation. If you have *believed* that you still were that old man, you may have acted like him. But that's not who you are. Now that you know who you are, you will find the power to behave in a way which is consistent with your true identity. Now it is a matter of renewing your mind to the truth so that your lifestyle will be transformed (Romans 12:2).

You Have a New Power over Sin

Before Jesus died and left you this spiritual fortune, you had no power to overcome sin. You sinned because you had no choice. It was your nature to do so. Now things have changed. You have a new nature—His! Because His life is within you, He will enable you to overcome sin as you depend on Him. Remember that the person you used to be, who loved to sin, has died (Romans 6:1-6). You were placed on the cross in Jesus Christ and crucified there with Him. Not only did He die, but *you* died too so that your life now consists of *Christ* in you (Galatians 2:20). "For he who has died is freed from sin" (Romans 6:7). To experience power over sin, simply rest in the sufficiency of Jesus Christ at every moment and continually affirm that you are *dead* to sin. Whether you feel it or not, "consider [yourself] to be dead to sin, but alive to God in Christ Jesus" (Romans 6:11). Just *act* like it's true because it is! When you depend on Jesus and act in faith, you will see for yourself that you *are* dead to sin.

Imagine Leo overdosing on cocaine and dying. They take his body to a funeral home and prepare it for burial. A few hours before the funeral starts, one of his drug buddies comes into the parlor where they have Leo's corpse laid out. Nobody else is in the room, so his buddy walks over to the casket and leans over. "Hey, Leo," he says, "we're alone right now, man. I've got some good stuff here in my pocket." He reaches into his pocket and pulls out a small bag with cocaine in it. "Look man, it's pure. Take a snort," he says, while putting the bag under Leo's nose. "What's your problem, man? Here, I'll put a little on my finger for you to taste. You'll see, it's good stuff."

Do you know what Leo's response is to all this? Nothing. He's just lying there. If Leo could speak at that moment, do you know what he would say? "Hey, stupid! I'm dead! Can't you see that?" Dead men don't want cocaine, even if they loved it before.

The Bible clearly teaches that a part of our inheritance is that we have *died* to sin. You can sin if you choose, but when you understand your new identity you will discover that you don't *want* to live in sin anymore. You died to all that. Now you are alive unto God. He motivates your desires and interests. You finally have power over sin!

You Have a New Freedom

You may have already known that your sin debt was paid by Jesus Christ, but if you haven't known your identity in Christ, you probably haven't experienced much freedom. When a Christian mistakenly believes that he is nothing more than a *sinner* saved by grace, he will wrap his life up in rules. He thinks that rules will produce a greater quality of spiritual living but, in reality, as Romans 7:10 tells us, religious rules always prove "to result in death." "A sinner saved by grace"—what a pitiful description of a person who possesses the very life of Jesus Christ! God prefers to call you a *saint*. That's how He refers to you 63 times in the New Testament. Why would a Christian want to identify himself by the word *sinner* when Jesus came to save him from his sin? God sees saints who sin, but He doesn't identify you as a sinner who is saved.

> *When a person knows God and the exceeding riches of His grace toward those of us who believe, he has entered into a lifestyle where grace rules.*

As you abide in Christ, you are free to do whatever you want. Paul said, "All things are lawful for me, but not all things are profitable" (1 Corinthians 6:12). This kind of statement almost scares a legalist to death. "I am free to do whatever I want?" That's right. *Abide in Christ* and do whatever you want to do.

What would happen if the spirit of Babe Ruth suddenly came into you? Do you suppose that you might find yourself overwhelmed with the desire to become a professional ballet dancer? Babe Ruth in tights—it's a scary thought. If wagers were placed on what you would do if the spirit of Babe possessed you, the odds wouldn't be high on the chance that you would take up ballet. It just doesn't fit. I think we all know what you *would* want to do.

As you enjoy intimacy with Jesus, you don't have to worry about religious rules. A legalist is afraid that if he doesn't build his life around rules then he will suddenly find himself consumed with a desire to live a lifestyle of sin. He needs to understand the implications of the fact that the Holy Spirit possesses him. His new nature has become one with the Holy Spirit so that when he is by faith walking in the spirit, *God's* desires become *his* desires. A person possessed with the Holy Spirit no more wants to live a lifestyle of continuous sin than one possessed with Babe's spirit wants to take up a lifestyle of ballet. God's plan is for the believer to trust the Holy Spirit to animate his behavior. He doesn't need rules, but enjoys real freedom. He has received "a spirit of wisdom and of revelation in the knowledge of Him" (Ephesians 1:17). When a person knows Him and the exceeding riches of His grace toward those of us who believe, he has entered into a lifestyle where grace rules.

• • •

Dear Father,
I want to experience the effect of the complete gospel. Open the eyes of my heart so that I may know the hope of Your calling and the riches of the glory of Your inheritance in me! I want to know the surpassing greatness of Your power in me. Don't stop until I fully know who I am in You! I want to experience everything of You that can be known in this lifetime.

G.R.A.C.E. Group Questions

1. Discuss the differences between a partial understanding of the gospel and the complete gospel. List four truths which you believe are typically missing from an incomplete presentation of the gospel.

2. Why did Jesus come into this world? What are the negative results present in the life of a person whose understanding of salvation goes no further than receiving forgiveness and going to heaven?

3. Read Colossians 1:25-28 and discuss what it means to *fully* carry out the preaching of the Word of God. What is the mystery that has been hidden from the ages?

4. What happened to your old identity at the time of your salvation? What would you tell a Christian who says, "I have been a drug addict all my life"?

5. Read Romans 6:1-7. What does it mean to be dead to sin? If we are dead to sin, why do Christians still sin? What is God's method for enabling us to experience victory over sin?

6. Steve suggests: "*Abide in Christ* and do whatever you want to do." What is your opinion about this kind of statement? How would you respond to a person who argues that this kind of advice can encourage people to sin?

10
Let's Party!

AFTER RESIGNING the pastorate to teach Grace Walk conferences, our family found itself in a situation we had never faced. Because I had been a pastor since the age of 19, we had always attended the church where God had called me to serve as pastor. But now it was necessary for us to select a church. Now we needed to find a church that our family could call home.

During our search, we visited one church that reeked of spiritual death. The problem wasn't their form of worship; I've seen God reveal Himself in churches that practiced many different forms of worship. The problem at this particular place was the absence of life. A person could easily conclude by the tone of the service that they had just received late-breaking news: It was all a big mistake. Jesus didn't rise from the dead after all. Sorry, folks. Have you ever been in a spiritually dead church service? If so, you know exactly what I am describing.

After the service ended, our family went to a local pizza restaurant. When we walked in the front door, a friendly greeter welcomed us. As we sat down at a table, I was struck by the cheerful atmosphere in the place. People were smiling and laughing together. Some were singing along with the mechanical characters that were on the stage to entertain the children. Our server was outgoing and seemed anxious to make our visit an enjoyable one. I found my mood being elevated just by being there.

Later as I thought about our experiences that morning, I concluded one thing: I had no interest at all in becoming a part of the church we had attended, but if the restaurant had given an invitation, I might have moved my membership there! The staff there seemed to enjoy life. They seemed to care about our needs. No doubt about it—they could have made a Pizzabyterian out of me that day!

The Party Poopers

The seventeenth-century reformers said that "man's chief end is to glorify God and enjoy Him forever." Enjoying God is an integral part of the life of one in whom grace rules. Legalism knows little about *enjoying* God and resents those who do. Do you remember the attitude of the older brother in the story of the prodigal son? The prodigal had gone to the far country and wasted his inheritance on wild living. When he came to his senses and returned home, his dad received him back with enthusiasm and joy. He threw a party in his honor.

Luke describes the reaction of the legalist in this story:

> Now [the] older son was in the field, and
> when he came and approached the house, he
> heard music and dancing. And he summoned
> one of the servants and began inquiring what
> these things might be. And he said to him,

"Your brother has come and your father has
killed the fattened calf, because he has received
him back safe and sound." But he became
angry, and was not willing to go in . . . (Luke
15:25-28).

There is no bigger party pooper than a legalist. He is
so focused on performance that he can't understand the
kind of grace that would cause a father to receive a person
whose activity hadn't been as admirable as his own. He
relates to others with a condescending attitude, judging
them by the standard of his own life. His performance
may look good, but inwardly he is wasting away because
his legalism has robbed him of authentic joy in the Christian life. He has no time for music and dancing; there's
work to be done! The devil never takes a break, why
should he? A legalist is never a genuinely happy person.
When he sees others dance to the music, he can't stand it.

The father of the prodigal said,
"We had to be merry and rejoice, for
this brother of yours was dead
and has begun to live."

This older brother bore the chief characteristics of a
legalist. First, he separated himself from his younger
brother because the latter didn't live up to the standards
embraced by himself. He refused to be involved in the same
party as his brother. Second, his relationship to his father
revolved around doing the right thing and not breaking his
commandments. He said, "For so many years I have been
serving you, and I never neglected a command of yours"
(Luke 15:29). He knew no intimacy with his father because

his whole focus was on behavior. Finally, he resented the grace that his father showed to the prodigal. He pointed out his own faithfulness and said, "When this son of yours came, who has devoured your wealth with harlots, you killed the fattened calf for him." Legalists sometimes find it hard to even call one a *brother* who doesn't conform to their own standards. The elder son called him "this son of yours." Such legalists apparently believe it's wrong to unconditionally accept a sinning Christian. After all, when we do so, we are condoning his behavior!

Fun Faith

The attitude of this elder brother reflects that held by legalists today. Yet the heart of the prodigal's father seems to parallel that of our Heavenly Father. He loves to celebrate when someone comes to him in full repentance. Faith and fun are not in opposition to one another; even under the old covenant, God made provision for His people to celebrate.

> You shall eat in the presence of the LORD your God, at the place where He chooses to establish His name, the tithe of all your grain, your new wine, your oil, and the first-born of your herd and your flock, in order that you may learn to fear the LORD your God always. . . . And you may spend the money for whatever your heart desires, for oxen, or sheep, or wine, or strong drink, or whatever your heart desires; and there you shall eat in the presence of the LORD your God and rejoice, you and your household (Deuteronomy 14:23,26).

Contrary to the opinion of some people, God loves fun! In eternity past, the three Persons of the Trinity all enjoyed intimacy with each other. It was a private party among the Father, Son, and Holy Spirit. Back then, before the foundation of time, God determined to host a universal party. It was to be a party in honor of His Son, Jesus. He would create man for the purpose of sharing His life with him, thus bringing him into the eternal party taking place in the heavenlies. And today, the Holy Spirit is involved in inviting people to come to the party. We could, in a sense, say that Christianity is a party celebrating Jesus Christ.

The father of the prodigal said, "We had to be merry and rejoice, for this brother of yours was dead and has begun to live" (Luke 15:32). When a dead person comes to life, that's a reason to celebrate. The Bible teaches in Ephesians 2:1 that there was a time when "you were dead in your trespasses and sins," but now you have been made alive by Jesus Christ. This is a reason to celebrate!

Some Christians today seem to have forgotten that the activity of the early church revolved around *fellowship*. The Greek word for that is *koinonia*. It wouldn't be inappropriate to use the word *party* as a contemporary paraphrase of the word. Many contemporary parties celebrate life: A birthday party celebrates the years a person has lived; anniversary parties celebrate a couple's life together; a graduation party celebrates the start of a new life for the graduate. Parties are focused on and full of life. Doesn't that description describe New Testament Christianity as well? Its essence is a celebration of divine life. You were dead, but in Christ Jesus you have been made alive! It's appropriate to "shout joyfully to the LORD" and to "serve the LORD with gladness" (Psalm 100:1-2). In other words, it's time for the church to rise up and have a party! Where grace rules, celebration is the order of the day.

Parties Attract People

The growth of the early church in Acts is inseparably linked to the fact that these early Christians continuously integrated celebration as a part of their daily lifestyle. They were consumed with an explosive joy that could not be squelched. Their lifestyle was an ongoing celebration of Jesus.

> Day by day continuing with one mind in the temple, and breaking bread from house to house, they were taking their meals together *with gladness and sincerity of heart* (Acts 2:46, emphasis added).

The early church had an uninhibited, exhilarating enthusiasm about Jesus Christ. On the day of Pentecost, when the Holy Spirit came upon the believers, they exhibited such excitement that onlookers stood in absolute "amazement and great perplexity, saying to one another, 'What does this mean?' But others were mocking and saying, 'They are full of sweet wine'" (Acts 2:12-13).

But the Christians were not drunk on wine; they were totally intoxicated with the life of Christ being expressed through them by the Holy Spirit. They were experiencing exactly what Paul meant when he said, "Do not get drunk with wine, for that is dissipation, but be filled with the Spirit" (Ephesians 5:18). These Christians partied "under the influence" of God's Holy Spirit all the time! They celebrated the life of Jesus in everything they did.

Ken spoke with me one day about how he had been considering resigning from his job and preparing to enter pastoral ministry. "Do you believe that God is calling you to make that kind of change?" I asked. "Well, it just makes sense to me," he answered. "I want my life to count for Christ. I think it would be good if I were in a job where I could do more *spiritual* things. My work as a salesman doesn't give me that many opportunities for spiritual activities." As we discussed his plans in depth, it became apparent that he believed that the activity of a pastor was more spiritual than that of a salesman.

> The early church
> helped win many people to Christ
> because they were so
> in love with Jesus.

Ken was mistaken, however. Our activity is *always* spiritual when it is animated by the life of Jesus Christ within us. A salesman who is totally depending on Jesus to control him will be as involved in spiritual activity as a pastor preaching in church on Sunday morning. In fact, compared to a pastor who preaches from his own self-sufficiency, a salesman's activity could actually be *more* spiritual!

It's not the deed, but the *source* of the deed that makes an action a spiritual one. Every Christian has the opportunity to celebrate Jesus in *every* activity of life. Anything we can't trust Jesus to perform through us shouldn't be done. If it is an action which the Lord empowers, then it is a godly action. Our society needs more men like Ken who will go into the marketplace and demonstrate what a man intoxicated with Jesus looks like.

Contemporary man is tired of stale religion. But when unbelievers see a person who has a consuming passion for

Jesus, he sits up and takes notice. A celebrating Christian will draw many people to come to Christ; people just can't resist a party. The early church helped win many people to Christ because they were so in love with Jesus. They proclaimed Him with unrestrained joy. They understood that Christ wasn't just a *part* of their life; He *was* their life!

Living Under the Influence

It is interesting that the apostle Paul linked the effects of alcohol and the influence of the Holy Spirit in the same verse. Drunkenness is a prominent part of many parties in our society. Yet in Ephesians 5:18, Paul asserted that Christians are not to be possessed by the power of alcohol, but rather are to surrender the control of their faculties to the influence of the Holy Spirit. The onlookers on the day of Pentecost made this same association when they accused the believers of being drunk on wine. Consider these characteristics of one who is "under the influence":

• *A Person Under the Influence Loses All Inhibitions.* Have you ever seen someone try to calm a drunk who is excited? It's almost impossible to do it. He *can't* be silenced. Such is the case when a person is filled with the Holy Spirit and a love for Jesus Christ. Evangelism is an excitement about Jesus which is contagious. When a person is overwhelmed by His grace, nothing can stop him from witnessing to others. When Peter and John were beaten and commanded not to witness anymore, they responded by saying, "We cannot stop speaking what we have seen and heard" (Acts 4:20). When the contemporary church becomes obsessed with Jesus Christ above everything else in life, nothing will be able to suppress the power of our witness.

• *A Person Under the Influence Becomes Very Expressive.* People under the influence of alcohol typically become more animated in their behavior. An angry drunk may begin to behave in a belligerent way. A happy person who is intoxicated may begin to act *very* happy. Alcohol seems to magnify the underlying trait that a person is exhibiting. When a person is governed by the grace of God, the One who is within him is magnified by the Holy Spirit. Walking in grace means that the Holy Spirit of God causes the believer to behave in a way which reveals the godliness of his inner character. He begins to express the life of Jesus Christ within him with unrestrained expression. The indwelling nature of Christ within the saint is magnified through his behavior when he acts under the influence of the Holy Spirit.

Lighten Up!

Our God is a party God! Those who feel that the idea of Christians "partying" seems somehow irreverent might benefit from a study of what the Bible says about joy in the kingdom of God. The Lord said, "My servants shall shout for joy" (Isaiah 65:14)! One of the last things Jesus told His disciples concerned having a festive heart: "These things I have spoken to you, that My joy may be in you, and that your joy may be made full" (John 15:11). In His final prayer before going to the cross, Jesus prayed "that they may have My joy made full in themselves" (John 17:13).

May the church once again rise up in celebration! We have been forgiven of our sins (Ephesians 1:7). Jesus Christ is our very life (Colossians 3:4). Nothing can separate us from the love of God (Romans 8:35-39). We will always triumph in life (2 Corinthians 2:14). It's time to lighten up and party!

Complete the following sentence: Jeremiah was a _____ . If your answer is "bullfrog," you're thinking of the wrong party! Jeremiah was a *prophet*. In fact, he is remembered as the weeping prophet. He apparently has many distant relatives in the modern church. They could sing, "Jeremiah was a prophet, he is a good friend of mine; I don't really remember a word he said; but like him I know how to whine." What a contrast with the prayer of Jesus, who asked for His church to have *joy*.

> *Paul wonderfully demonstrated that a person can experience joy without happiness.*

There is a tragic lack of joy in the lives of many believers today because they are willing to settle for happiness. Happiness depends on *happenings*. A person is happy when the circumstances of life are to his liking. While pursuing happiness is the primary goal for many Christians, it isn't a high priority to God for us to be happy. He wants to give us *joy*. Happiness depends on external circumstances; joy runs much deeper than that. Happiness comes from the outside into us, but joy comes from the inside out. It is a pleasure that flows from our innermost being—an inner sense of well-being and contentment produced by an awareness of our union with Jesus Christ. Joy is unaffected by our surroundings.

Joy has no relationship to happiness. Consider Paul's time in the jail at Philippi. He wasn't happy to be there. He said that he had "the desire to depart and be with Christ, for that is very much better" (Philippians 1:23). Jail was no thrill for him. Yet the theme of his letter to the Philippians was that of rejoicing. Repeatedly he echoes the message "rejoice in the Lord" (Philippians 3:1). In prison, Paul might not have felt the happiness that circumstances provide, but he definitely experienced the joy that comes from intimacy with Jesus Christ. He understood that "to live is Christ, and to die is gain" (Philippians 1:21). His life wasn't joined to the external, but the Eternal. He wonderfully demonstrated that a person can experience joy without happiness. The world will never know more than transient happiness, which comes and goes with the winds of circumstance. By contrast, a man in Christ can experience joy at all times.

Are you in Christ? Then join the party. God won't mind. In fact, He has been waiting for you to enjoy the celebration. Go ahead and let go. Believe it, live it, sing it. *Celebrate! Celebrate! Dance to the music of His grace!*

• • •

Dear Father,

I have allowed myself to become too rigid, too uptight. I want to experience the joy of my union with You. Free me from everything that keeps me from joining the party. I want to celebrate the life of Jesus continually. By faith, I receive the fullness of joy which Jesus prayed that His followers would possess. May that joy overflow from my life so that others may be drawn to You because of me.

G.R.A.C.E. Group Questions

1. "Man's chief end is to glorify God and enjoy Him forever." Discuss what it means to enjoy God. Is it possible to glorify God without enjoying Him? Identify some practical ways that a Christian may both glorify and enjoy Him.

2. Read the story of the elder brother in Luke 15:25-32. List the three characteristics of legalism reflected in this son's life which are mentioned in this chapter. What other characteristics of legalism are demonstrated by his attitude and actions? Can you identify with any of these characteristics?

3. Identify the elements of a party which are presented in Psalm 100. What other passages in the Bible illustrate the celebration that exists in the kingdom of God?

4. Identify verses in Acts which show people being drawn to the church because of the celebration that existed among the Christians there.

5. Read Ephesians 5:18 and Acts 2:12,13. What similarities do we see between being under the influence of alcohol

and under the control of the Holy Spirit? Discuss three other similarities not mentioned in these passages.

6. How can it be proven from the Bible that God is "a party God"? Identify verses in the book of Revelation which indicate that a party is happening there continuously.

7. Define *happiness* and *joy*. What are the differences between the two? Can you think of a time in your life when you experienced joy but were not happy?

11

Grace Rules!

THERE *MUST* BE MORE to the Christian life than what I am experiencing!" Over the past two decades, I've heard statements like that expressed in one way or another many times. For years I felt the same way. While I was deeply grateful for God's forgiveness toward my sins, I recognized that my own experience was very much different from that of the Christians described in the New Testament. I viewed the gospel as good news that told a man how to get into heaven, but it seemed to possess little ability to get heaven into a man. The gospel had great relevance in terms of eternity, but seemed to offer little hope for experiencing life to the fullest while still in this world.

In an effort to inject life into my circumstances, I would often increase the level of my religious activity. I was like a man adrift at sea, drinking the salt water of the surrounding ocean only to discover that the more he drinks, the thirstier he becomes. Such is the fate of anyone who seeks to find fulfillment in religious performance.

Regardless of a person's particular brand, religion can *never* satisfy his deepest longings.

I assume that your commitment of time and effort in reading this book indicates a personal hunger to more fully experience the grace of God. If you too believe that there must be more to the Christian life than you are experiencing, there is! Fulfillment will no more be found through a religious identity than any other faulty efforts to be fulfilled. Authentic contentment can be found only in Jesus Christ. He alone is able to rescue the believer stranded in the sea of religious regiment void of divine life. When grace rules in a believer's life, the result will be evident in several ways.

Grace Energizes the Christian

Nothing is more invigorating to the life of a believer than continuously experiencing the grace of God. Religion drains a person. A religious man is a driven man. By contrast, grace doesn't drive us, but *directs* us in a way that we enjoy serving God from a heart filled with gratitude. A person walking in grace becomes increasingly energized as he serves, not spiritually exhausted. Although he may at times experience the normal fatigue of mind and body that is common to humanity, he discovers that inwardly he is constantly empowered by divine life. His "inner man is being renewed day by day" (2 Corinthians 4:16). He finds himself motivated from within to serve Jesus Christ with enthusiasm and consistency.

License to Be Lazy?

"I don't have to do anything because I'm under grace," Becky said. She and her husband had disagreed many times about the responsibility of a Christian walking in grace. "I believe that there are certain things we need to do and grace has nothing to do with it," he argued. They had come to me to settle the question for them. What would you tell them if they asked your opinion on the matter? Does a Christian have a duty to do certain things or is he free to sit down and do nothing for the rest of his life?

It's true that grace delivers the believer from the realm of religious duty. Becky wasn't wrong in her assertion that Christians don't have to do anything. However, during the course of my conversation with this couple, I sensed that neither of them clearly understood what it means to walk in grace. Becky's husband was trying to impose his religious expectations on her. There was no doubt about that. On the other hand, Becky didn't appear to be on target in her perspective on the matter either. It sounded as if she had indeed become passive in many ways.

> *A grace-filled Christian usually won't meet the expectations of the legalist, but at the same time he won't become lazy in his Christian walk.*

The good news of grace doesn't stop by causing a person to understand that he is free from the law. Genuine grace not only delivers us *from* something, but also delivers us *to* Someone. Grace opens our eyes to the union we share with Jesus Christ. It doesn't give the believer an excuse to become lethargic and lazy. Instead, it energizes him with the divine life of Jesus in such a way that he serves God with supernatural power. Grace is the divine enablement for one to powerfully express the life of Jesus Christ through his lifestyle.

Jesus' Power in You

Jesus was full of grace (see John 1:14). In three short years, His activity had influenced the whole known world because His actions were impregnated with divine power. That's hardly a description of a passive person. Concerning the lifestyle of those who follow Him, John said that "of His fullness we have all received, and grace upon grace" (John 1:16). God has poured the grace of Jesus Christ into us in a manner that causes us to be filled with grace. Our lives are piled high with grace on top of grace!

Possessing the power of Jesus Christ, why would any Christian want to become passive? A person who suggests that the message of grace will produce passivity simply doesn't understand what it means to walk in grace. A believer who has become passive hasn't experienced the reality of grace ruling in his life. A grace-filled Christian usually won't meet the expectations of the legalist, but at the same time he won't become lazy in his Christian walk. His lifestyle is a grace *walk*. Walking is always progressive, not passive.

The Spirit of Jesus dwells within the believer. An understanding of the implications of that truth will mobilize the believer. If the essence of Mozart suddenly came into you, what would you want to do? If the spirit of Picasso possessed you, would it make sense to never pick up a paint brush? If you were possessed by the life force of Mozart, nothing could keep you away from a piano. You would be thrilled by the awareness of the ability you possessed and would want to express it often. The knowledge of who was within you would be all the motivation you needed.

The good news of grace is that *Jesus Christ is in you.* What an awesome thought! You are privileged to live in a day that Old Testament saints couldn't even imagine.

They were thrilled when they met God on a mountain, in a burning bush, or through a pillar of fire or a cloud of glory. These occasional encounters with Deity were often enough to change a man's life forever. These people had only a fleeting glimpse of His glory, and yet they were transformed.

On the day that Jesus was crucified, the front door to the bank of heaven swung open wide and all the glory of God came pouring out over all those who received Him. The glory vault of heaven was opened and emptied out on every believer! This concept was an unknown mystery in the Old Testament, but you belong to a chosen group "to whom God willed to make known what is the riches of the glory of this mystery among the Gentiles, which is Christ in you, the hope of glory" (Colossians 1:27).

If the Old Testament saints were so greatly motivated by a rare glimpse of God, what impact can the resident glory of God in the New Testament believer have on his life and the lives of those around him? When a person knows who he is in Jesus Christ, he will be forever transformed. Once the revelation of the indwelling Christ becomes a reality to him it can never be *unknown* again. He will never get over the impact of seeing Jesus in him, of knowing that Christ is his very life. He will be forever energized by the glory of Christ within him.

Grace Promotes Spiritual Reality

I'm not a religious man anymore. God rescued me from that when I began to understand what it means to experience the reality of my identity in Jesus Christ. I don't mean to suggest that I have abandoned all the behavior that marked my lifestyle before I understood the grace walk. I still do many of the same things I have always done. I still pray and preach, read my Bible, and go to church. The difference now is the *source* of my behavior. Whereas my actions as a legalist reflected *my* efforts to serve God, I have come to learn what it means to act in the power of *His* divine effort. As grace rules in my life, I find that activity which once was empty is now an exuberant expression of Christ's life. I now enjoy doing the things that at one time were duty.

It's exciting to know that spiritual service is not our gift to God, but rather His gift to us. Paul described the nature of Christian service in Ephesians 2:10: "We are His workmanship, created in Christ Jesus *for good works, which God prepared beforehand, that we should walk in them*" (emphasis added). As a legalist, I viewed service as an obligation I had toward God. I thought it was my duty to produce behavior that would glorify Him. Consequently, I found it necessary to identify those things which I believed would please Him.

Yet when grace began to rule my life, my perspective changed completely. I began to understand what Paul meant when he described how God has *in advance* prepared good works in which Christians may participate. A person walking in grace doesn't get up each day with resolve to serve the Lord. He simply chooses to abide in Christ, moves forward through his day, and when he sees an opportunity to serve God, he rejoices that the omnipotent God of the universe allows him to participate in what God is doing in this world. "Great!" he may say. "Look at the good work that God has prepared for me today! Thank You, Lord, that I am able to join You in Your work in this world!" In the spiritual reality of a grace walk, service is the natural expression of who we are.

Effective, meaningful Christian service is never inspired by rules. Only the grace of God can enable a person to live a lifestyle which glorifies Him. Paul reminded Titus of this truth, saying, "The grace of God has appeared, bringing salvation to all men, instructing us to deny ungodliness and worldly desires and to live sensibly, righteously and godly in the present age" (Titus 2:11-12). God's grace both inspires and instructs us in godly living.

By the cross of Jesus,
you have been set free from
the dungeon of duty
and have been brought into
the light of liberty in Christ.

The kingdom of God is not a kingdom of rules, but of relationship. Writing to the Christians at Rome who argued about whether it was right to drink this or that, or to eat one thing or another, Paul asserted that "the kingdom of God is not eating and drinking, but righteousness and peace and joy in the Holy Spirit" (Romans 14:17). The focal point of authentic faith is Jesus Christ, not a list of do's and don'ts. Intimacy with Him will facilitate behavior which is holy. Continually experiencing His grace will never encourage sin, but will always promote godly living. Paul said, "Sin shall not be master over you, for you are not under law, but under grace" (Romans 6:14). The grace of God and the person of Christ are synonymous. When God's grace is functioning through a man, his actions will be an expression of the indwelling Christ.

Welcome to the Kingdom

For 29 years after I became a Christian I didn't understand how God intended for me to live. I wanted to glorify Him and sincerely tried to do what I believed He expected. Despite all my efforts, there was an ever-present sense that I was missing something. I believed that *surely* the death of Jesus was meant to produce more in a person's life than what I could see in mine. I believed that it probably was impossible to experience consistent victory and to feel truly fulfilled in this lifetime. I was a man wandering in spiritual shadows, getting only an occasional glimpse of the light of liberty.

I lived under the domain of law, with a paradigm for life that didn't allow for the kind of exhilarating lifestyle I now know is possible to anyone who is in Christ. Paul said, "He delivered us from the domain of darkness, and transferred us to the kingdom of His beloved Son" (Colossians 1:13). The greatest discovery of my life since salvation was the day that the Holy Spirit opened my eyes to see what it means to live in the kingdom of His beloved Son.

Are you struggling under the dominion of rules? By the cross of Jesus, you have been set free from the dungeon of duty and have been brought into the light of liberty in Christ. You are a citizen of this new kingdom. Come out into the light and enjoy your birthright! "It was for freedom that Christ set us free; therefore keep standing firm and do not be subject again to a yoke of slavery" (Galatians 5:1). The battle is over and you won because of Jesus. God has paid everything you owed. You can now live in carefree, total abandon in Him. You don't have to ever be afraid again. You never need to focus on yourself to see if you measure up. You don't live in the place where those things matter anymore. You are in the kingdom of Jesus Christ now! You can rejoice and rest— it is a kingdom where grace rules.

• • •

Dear Father,

Make it so in my own experience. I want grace to rule over me. I affirm that You are my life and from this day forward I will seek to know You above all else. May the revelation of who I am in You become increasingly real to me. Teach me how to walk in grace. Express your life through me and transform me by Your eternal love.

G.R.A.C.E. Group Questions

1. How would you respond to the person who says, "I don't have to do anything because I'm under grace"? How would you encourage a Christian who seems to be spiritually lazy?

2. Read John 1:14-17. Paraphrase this passage in your own words. In what ways was it evident in the earthly ministry of Jesus that He was full of grace and truth? What is the difference between being full of grace and full of truth?

3. On a number of occasions in the Old Testament, God revealed Himself to people. Which account of such revelations is your favorite? Explain the mystery among the Gentiles that Paul mentions in Colossians 1:27. How have you seen the glory of God in your own life?

4. List three differences between empty religion and spiritual reality.

5. Read Ephesians 2:10 and explain what the Bible means when it says that God has already prepared good works in which we are to walk. How does this verse reveal God's grace as it relates to works?

6. Read Titus 2:11-12. How does grace teach us to deny ungodliness? How does it instruct us in godly living?

7. Describe the main characteristics of living in the kingdom of God's dear Son. How does living in the kingdom of grace differ from the domain of law?

A Personal Word

If your life has been influenced by reading *Grace Rules*, I would be happy to hear from you. Grace Walk Ministries offers a Grace Walk Conference in which information about the identity of the believer and teaching on law and grace are presented in an expanded form. We also offer other conferences that focus on how grace affects various areas of the Christian life. If you are interested in receiving information about my teaching and preaching ministry or about Grace Walk Ministries, please feel free to contact me at the following address:

Dr. Steve McVey
Grace Walk Ministries
PO Box 725368
Atlanta, GA 31139-9368
Phone: 800/472-2311
E-mail: gracewalk@aol.com
Website: www.gracewalk.org

May God continue to bless you in your own grace walk as you come to "know Him, and the power of His resurrection and the fellowship of His sufferings" (Philippians 3:10).

WHAT YOU'VE ALWAYS WANTED IN THE CHRISTIAN LIFE...

Grace Walk

STEVE McVEY

Nothing you have ever done, nothing you could ever do, will match the incomparable joy of letting Jesus live His life through you. It is what makes the fire of passion burn so brightly in new believers. And it is what causes the light of contentment to dance in the eyes of mature believers who have learned the secret of the Grace Walk.

If you know how to live it, you'll be strengthened by the depth of Steve McVey's insights. If you long for it, you can begin today!

Other Good
Harvest House Reading

LIFETIME GUARANTEE
by *Bill Gillham*

You've tried fixing your marriage, your kids, your job. Suddenly the light dawns. It's not your problems that need fixing, it's your *life!* The key to experiencing victory in Christ lies in learning how to literally "walk in newness of life" as described in the Word. Guaranteed.

VICTORY OVER DEPRESSION
by *Bob George*

This book offers practical help to anyone who is experiencing disappointment or depression as a result of poor relationships, past mistakes, personal tragedies, career or financial struggles, or illness.

GRACE LAND
by *Steve McVey*

Using Israel's wilderness journey and promised land arrival, Steve reveals God's persistence in fulfilling His promises. Christians are encouraged to enter the land of grace and live in God's strength. Includes prayers and discussion questions.